Also by Patrick Lencioni

Leadership Fables
The Five Temptations of a CEO
The Four Obsessions of an Extraordinary Executive
Death by Meeting
Silos, Politics, and Turf Wars

Field Guide
Overcoming the Five Dysfunctions of a Team

The Five Dysfunctions of a Team

A LEADERSHIP FABLE

Patrick Lencioni

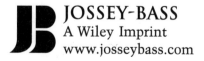

JOSSEY-BASS
A Wiley Imprint
www.josseybass.com

Published by Jossey-Bass
A Wiley Imprint
989 Market Street, San Francisco, CA 94103-1741   www.josseybass.com

Jossey-Bass books and products are available through most bookstores. To contact Jossey-Bass directly call our Customer Care Department within the U.S. at 800-956-7739, outside the U.S. at 317-572-3986, or fax 317-572-4002.

Jossey-Bass also publishes its books in a variety of electronic formats. Some content that appears in print may not be available in electronic books.

Library of Congress Cataloging-in-Publication Data
Lencioni, Patrick, 1965–
    The five dysfunctions of a team : a leadership fable / Patrick Lencioni.
      p. cm.
    ISBN 0-7879-6075-6
    1. Teams in the workplace. I. Title.
    HD66 .L456 2002
    658.4'036—dc21   2001008099

Printed in the United States of America
FIRST EDITION
HB Printing   30 29 28 27 26 25 24 23 22 21

CONTENTS

To Dad, for teaching me the value of work.
And to Mom, for encouraging me to write.

INTRODUCTION

Not finance. Not strategy. Not technology. It is teamwork that remains the ultimate competitive advantage, both because it is so powerful and so rare.

A friend of mine, the founder of a company that grew to a billion dollars in annual revenue, best expressed the power of teamwork when he once told me, "If you could get all the people in an organization rowing in the same direction, you could dominate any industry, in any market, against any competition, at any time."

Whenever I repeat that adage to a group of leaders, they immediately nod their heads, but in a desperate sort of way. They seem to grasp the truth of it while simultaneously surrendering to the impossibility of actually making it happen.

And that is where the rarity of teamwork comes into play. For all the attention that it has received over the years from scholars, coaches, teachers, and the media, teamwork is as elusive as it has ever been within most organizations. The fact remains that teams, because they are made up of imperfect human beings, are inherently dysfunctional.

But that is not to say that teamwork is doomed. Far from it. In fact, building a strong team is both possible and remarkably simple. But it is painfully difficult.

That's right. Like so many other aspects of life, teamwork comes down to mastering a set of behaviors that are at once theoretically uncomplicated, but extremely difficult to put into practice day after day. Success comes only for those groups that overcome the all-too-human behavioral tendencies that corrupt teams and breed dysfunctional politics within them.

As it turns out, these principles apply to more than just teamwork. In fact, I stumbled upon them somewhat by accident in my pursuit of a theory about leadership.

A few years ago I wrote my first book, *The Five Temptations of a CEO,* about the behavioral pitfalls that plague leaders. In the course of working with my clients, I began to notice that some of them were "misusing" my theories in an effort to assess and improve the performance of their leadership *teams*—and with success!

And so it became apparent to me that the five temptations applied not only to individual leaders but, with a few modifications, to groups as well. And not just within corporations. Clergy, coaches, teachers, and others found that these principles applied in their worlds as much as they did in the executive suite of a multinational company. And that is how this book came to be.

Like my other books, *The Five Dysfunctions of a Team* begins with a story written in the context of a realistic but fictional organization. I have found that this allows readers to learn more effectively by losing themselves in a story and by being able to relate to the characters. It also helps them understand how these principles can be applied in a nontheoretical, real-world environment, where the pace of work and the volume of daily distractions make even the simplest of tasks seem arduous.

In order to help you apply the material in your own organization, a brief section following the story outlines the five dysfunctions in detail. That section also includes a team assessment and suggested tools for overcoming the issues that might be plaguing your team.

Finally, although this book is based on my work with CEOs and their executive teams, its theories are applicable for anyone interested in teamwork, whether you lead a small department within a company or are simply a member of a team that could use some improvement. Whatever the case may be, I sincerely hope it helps your team overcome its particular dysfunctions so that it can achieve more than individuals could ever imagine doing alone. That, after all, is the real power of teamwork.

The Fable

LUCK

Only one person thought Kathryn was the right choice to become CEO of DecisionTech, Inc. Luckily for her, that person was the Chairman of the board.

And so, less than a month after the previous chief executive had been removed, Kathryn Petersen took the reins of a company that just two years earlier had been one of the most talked-about, well-funded, and promising start-up companies in the recent history of the Silicon Valley. She could not have known just how far from grace the company had fallen in such a short period of time, and what the next few months had in store for her.

PART ONE

Under–achievement

BACKSTORY

DecisionTech was located in Half Moon Bay, a foggy, coastal farming town just over the hills from the San Francisco Bay. It was not technically part of the Silicon Valley, but the Valley is not so much a geographical entity as a cultural one. And DecisionTech certainly fit within that world.

It had the most experienced—and expensive—executive team imaginable, a seemingly indestructible business plan, and more top-tier investors than any young company could hope for. Even the most cautious venture firms were lining up to invest, and talented engineers were submitting their resumés before the company had leased an office.

But that was almost two years earlier, which is a lifetime for a technology start-up. After its first few euphoric months of existence, the company began experiencing a series of ongoing disappointments. Critical deadlines started to slip. A few key employees below the executive level unexpectedly left the company. Morale deteriorated gradually. All of this in spite of the considerable advantages that DecisionTech had amassed for itself.

On the two-year anniversary of the firm's founding, the board unanimously agreed to "ask" Jeff Shanley, the company's thirty-seven-year-old CEO and cofounder, to step down. He was offered the job of heading business development, and to the surprise of his colleagues, he accepted the demotion, not wanting to walk away from a potentially huge payout should the company eventually go public. And even in the difficult economic climate of the Valley, the company had every reason to go public.

None of DecisionTech's 150 employees were shocked by Jeff's removal. While most of them seemed to like him well enough personally, they couldn't deny that under his leadership the atmosphere within the company had become increasingly troubling. Backstabbing among the executives had become an art. There was no sense of unity or camaraderie on the team, which translated into a muted level of commitment. Everything seemed to take too long to get done, and even then it never felt right.

Some boards might have been more patient with a stumbling executive team. DecisionTech's was not. There was just too much at stake—and too high a profile—to watch the company waste away because of politics. DecisionTech had already developed a reputation within the Valley for being one of the most political and unpleasant places to work, and the board couldn't tolerate that kind of press, especially when the future had looked so promising just a couple of years earlier.

Someone had to be accountable for the mess, and Jeff was the man at the top. Everyone seemed relieved when the board announced the decision to remove him.

Until three weeks later, when Kathryn was hired.

KATHRYN

The executives couldn't agree on which of Kathryn's features presented the biggest problem. There were so many.

First, she was old. Ancient, at least by Silicon Valley standards. Kathryn was fifty-seven.

More important, she had no real high-tech experience other than serving as a board member of Trinity Systems, a large technology company in San Francisco. Most of her career had been spent in operational roles with decidedly low-tech companies, the most notable of which was an automobile manufacturer.

But more than her age or experience, Kathryn just didn't seem to fit the DecisionTech culture.

She had started her career in the military, then married a teacher and basketball coach at a local high school. After raising three boys, she taught seventh grade for a few years until she discovered her affinity for business.

At the age of thirty-seven, Kathryn enrolled in a three-year business school night program, which she completed a semester early at Cal State Hayward, which was not exactly Harvard or Stanford. She then spent the next fifteen years in and around manufacturing, until her retirement at the age of fifty-four.

The fact that Kathryn was a woman was never an issue for the executive team; two of them were women themselves. With much of their collective experience coming from the somewhat progressive world of high tech, most had worked for women at some time during their careers. But even if her gender had been a problem for anyone on the team, it would have been dwarfed by her glaring cultural mismatch.

There was just no mistaking the fact that, on paper, Kathryn was an old school, blue-collarish executive. That presented a stark contrast to the DecisionTech executives and middle managers, most of whom had little experience working outside of the Valley. Some of them even liked to brag that they hadn't worn a suit—outside of a wedding— since graduating from college.

It was no surprise that after first reading her resumé, board members questioned the Chairman's sanity when he suggested they hire Kathryn. But he eventually wore them down.

For one, the board believed their Chairman when he flat out assured them that Kathryn would succeed. Second, he had been known to have extremely good instincts about people, notwithstanding the problem with Jeff. He certainly wouldn't make two mistakes in a row, they reasoned.

But perhaps most important of all (though no one would

admit it), DecisionTech was in a desperate situation. The Chairman insisted that there weren't too many capable executives willing to take on such a messy job given the current state of affairs at the scarred company. "We should consider ourselves lucky to have such a capable leader as Kathryn available," he successfully argued.

Whether or not that was true, the Chairman was determined to hire someone he knew and could trust. When he called Kathryn to tell her about the job, he certainly could not have known that he would be regretting the decision just a few weeks later.

RATIONALE

No one was more surprised about the offer than Kathryn. Although she had known the Chairman for many years on a personal level (Kathryn had actually first met him when her husband coached his oldest son in high school), she could not have imagined that he thought so highly of her as an executive.

Most of their relationship had been social, centering around family, school, and local athletics. Kathryn assumed that the Chairman had little idea about her life outside her role as a mother and coach's wife.

In fact, the Chairman had followed Kathryn's career with interest over the years, amazed at how successful she had become with such relatively modest training. In less than five years, she had become chief operating officer of the Bay Area's only automobile manufacturing plant, a U.S.-Japanese joint venture. She held that job for the better part of a decade and made the plant one of the most successful cooperative enterprises in the country. And while the

Chairman knew little about the car industry, he knew one thing about Kathryn that convinced him she was perfect to fix the problems at DecisionTech.

She had an amazing gift for building teams.

GRUMBLINGS

I f the executives at DecisionTech had any doubts about Kathryn when her hiring was first announced—and they did—they were even more concerned after their new leader's first two weeks on the job.

It wasn't that Kathryn did anything controversial or misplaced. It was that she did almost nothing at all.

Aside from a brief reception on her first day and subsequent interviews with each of her direct reports, Kathryn spent almost all of her time walking the halls, chatting with staff members, and silently observing as many meetings as she could find time to attend. And perhaps most controversial of all, she actually asked Jeff Shanley to continue leading the weekly executive staff meetings, where she just listened and took notes.

The only real action that Kathryn took during those first weeks was to announce a series of two-day executive retreats in the Napa Valley to be held over the course of the next few months. As though she needed to give them any more ammunition, none of her reports could believe she had the gall to take them out of the office for so many days when there was so much real work to be done.

And to make matters worse, when someone suggested a specific topic for discussion during the first retreat, Kathryn refused. She had her own agenda already set.

Even the Chairman was surprised, and a bit unnerved, about the reports of Kathryn's early performance. He came to the conclusion that if she didn't work out, he should probably leave along with her. That was beginning to feel like the most probable outcome.

OBSERVATIONS

After her first two weeks observing the problems at DecisionTech, Kathryn had more than a few moments when she wondered if she should have taken the job. But she knew that there was little chance that she would have turned it down. Retirement had made her antsy, and nothing excited her more than a challenge.

While there was no doubt that DecisionTech would be a challenge, something seemed different about this one. Though she had never really feared failure, Kathryn could not deny that the prospect of letting the Chairman down spooked her a little. To tarnish her reputation so late in her career, and among friends and family, was enough to worry even the most secure of people. And Kathryn was certainly secure with herself.

After surviving a stint in the military, raising her boys, watching countless buzzer-beating basketball games, and standing up to union bosses, Kathryn decided she was not about to be intimidated by a bunch of harmless yuppies whose greatest hardships in life so far had been fighting off the first signs of a receding hairline or an expanding waistline. She believed that as long as the board would give her enough time and leeway, she would be able to turn DecisionTech around.

And Kathryn's lack of in-depth software experience did not concern her. In fact, she felt certain that it provided her with an advantage. Most of her staff seemed almost paralyzed by their own knowledge of technology, as though they themselves would have to do the programming and product design to make the company fly.

Kathryn knew that Jack Welch didn't have to be an expert on toaster manufacturing to make General Electric a success and that Herb Kelleher didn't have to spend a lifetime flying airplanes to build Southwest Airlines. Despite what her limited technical background might have indicated, Kathryn felt that her understanding of enterprise software and technology was more than sufficient for her to lead DecisionTech out of the mess it was in.

What she could not have known when she accepted the job, however, was just how dysfunctional her executive team was, and how they would challenge her in ways that no one before had ever done.

THE STAFF

Employees referred to the DecisionTech executives as The Staff. No one referred to them as a team, which Kathryn decided was no accident.

In spite of their undeniable intelligence and impressive educational backgrounds, The Staff's behavior during meetings was worse than anything she had seen in the automotive world. Though open hostility was never really apparent and no one ever seemed to argue, an underlying tension was undeniable. As a result, decisions never seemed to get made; discussions were slow and uninteresting, with few real exchanges; and everyone seemed to be desperately waiting for each meeting to end.

And yet, as bad as the team was, they all seemed like well-intentioned and reasonable people when considered individually. With just a few exceptions.

JEFF—FORMER CEO, BUSINESS DEVELOPMENT

Essentially a generalist who loved networking within the Valley, Jeff Shanley had raised a considerable amount of the company's initial money and attracted many of the current executives. No one could deny his prowess when it came to venture capital or recruiting. But management was another story.

Jeff ran staff meetings as though he were a student body president reading from a textbook on protocol. He always published an agenda before each meeting, and then distributed detailed minutes afterward. And unlike most other high-tech companies, his meetings usually began on time and always concluded exactly when they were scheduled to end. The fact that nothing ever seemed to get done during those meetings didn't appear to bother him.

In spite of his demotion, Jeff maintained his seat on the board of directors. Kathryn initially suspected that he might resent her for taking his job, but she soon came to the conclusion that Jeff was relieved to be, well, relieved of his management responsibilities. Kathryn had little concern about his presence on the board, or on her management team. She suspected that his heart was in the right place.

MIKEY—MARKETING

Marketing would be a critical function at DecisionTech, and the board had been ecstatic to get someone as sought after as Michele Bebe. Mikey, as she liked to be called, was well known throughout the Valley as a brand-building genius. Which made it all the more astonishing that she lacked a few key social graces.

During meetings, she talked more than the others, occasionally coming up with a brilliant idea, but more often complaining about how the other companies she had worked for did everything better than DecisionTech. It was almost as though she were a spectator or, better yet, a victim of circumstance, at her new company. Though she never argued outright with any of her peers, she was known to roll her eyes in apparent disgust when one of them disagreed with anything she had to say about marketing. Kathryn decided that Mikey was unaware of how she came across to others. No one would purposefully act that way, she reasoned.

So in spite of her talent and accomplishments, it was no surprise to Kathryn that Mikey was the least popular among the rest of the staff. With the possible exception of Martin.

MARTIN—CHIEF TECHNOLOGIST

A founder of the company, Martin Gilmore was the closest thing that DecisionTech had to an inventor. He had designed the original specs for the company's flagship product, and although others had done much of the actual product development, the executives often said that Martin was the keeper of the crown jewels. That analogy was due at least in part to the fact that Martin was British.

Martin considered himself to know as much about technology as anyone else in the Valley, which was probably true. With advanced degrees from Berkeley and Cambridge, and a track record of success as a chief architect at two other technology companies, he was seen as Decision-Tech's key competitive advantage, at least when it came to human capital.

Unlike Mikey, Martin didn't disrupt staff meetings. In fact, he rarely participated. It wasn't that he refused to attend those meetings (even Jeff wouldn't allow such a blatant act of revolt); it was just that he always had his laptop open, and he seemed to be constantly checking e-mail or doing something similarly engrossing. Only when someone made a factually incorrect statement could Martin be counted on to offer a comment, and usually a sarcastic one at that.

At first, this was tolerable, maybe even amusing, to Martin's peers, who seemed in awe of his intellect. But it began to wear on the staff over time. And with the company's recent struggles, it had become an increasingly grating source of frustration for many of them.

JR—SALES

In order to avoid confusing him with Jeff Shanley, everyone called the head of sales JR. His real name was Jeff Rawlins, but he seemed to enjoy the new moniker. JR was an experienced salesperson and a little older than the others—mid-forties. He was usually tan, never rude, and always agreed to do whatever the staff asked of him.

Unfortunately, JR rarely followed through. In those cases when he came clean and acknowledged having made a commitment that went unfulfilled, he apologized profusely to whomever he had let down.

In spite of what the staff called JR's flakiness, he was able to maintain a measure of respect from his peers because of his track record. Before coming to DecisionTech, he had never missed a quarterly revenue number in his entire career in sales.

CARLOS—CUSTOMER SUPPORT

Though DecisionTech had relatively few customers, the board felt strongly that the company would need to invest early in customer service in order to prepare for growth. Carlos Amador had worked with Mikey at two previous companies, and she introduced him to the firm. Which was ironic because the two of them couldn't have been more different.

Carlos spoke very little, but whenever he did, he had something important and constructive to say. He listened intently during meetings, worked long hours with no complaint, and downplayed his prior accomplishments whenever someone asked about them. If there was a low-maintenance member of the staff, and a trustworthy one, it was Carlos.

Kathryn was thankful not to have to worry about at least one of her new direct reports, although she was somewhat troubled that his specific role had not yet fully developed. The fact that he willingly took on responsibility for product quality and any other unattractive duties that fell through the gaps allowed her to focus on more pressing concerns.

JAN—CHIEF FINANCIAL OFFICER

The role of the chief financial officer had been a critical one at DecisionTech and would continue to be as long as the company intended to go public. Jan Mersino knew what she was getting into when she joined the company, and she had played a key role supporting Jeff as he raised impressive amounts of money from venture capitalists and other investors.

Jan was a stickler for detail, took pride in her knowledge of the industry, and treated the company's money as though it were her own. While the board had given Jeff and the staff virtual free rein when it came to expenditures, they did so only because they knew that Jan would not let things get out of control.

NICK—CHIEF OPERATING OFFICER

The final member of the executive staff was the most impressive on paper. Nick Farrell had been vice president of field operations for a large computer manufacturer in the Midwest, and had moved his family to California to take the DecisionTech job. Unfortunately for him, he had the most ill-defined role of anyone on the team.

Nick was officially the chief operating officer of the company, but that was only because he had demanded the COO title as a condition of accepting the job. Jeff and the board gave it to him because they believed he would earn it within the year anyway if he performed according to his billing. More importantly, they had become addicted to hiring star executives, and losing Nick would have hurt their winning percentage.

Of all the members of the executive staff, Nick had been most directly impacted by the company's sputtering start. Given Jeff's limitations as a manager, Nick had been hired to spearhead DecisionTech's growth, which included building an operational infrastructure, opening new offices around the world, and leading the firm's acquisition and integration efforts. Most of his responsibilities were currently on hold, giving Nick little meaningful day-to-day work.

As frustrated as he was, Nick didn't complain openly. To the contrary, he worked hard to build relationships, though sometimes shallow ones, with each of his colleagues, whom he had quietly deemed to be inferior to him. And though he certainly never said so to any of his peers, Nick felt he was the only executive in the company qualified to be CEO. But that would become obvious soon enough.

PART TWO

Lighting
the Fire

FIRST TEST

I t looked like just another of the many standard e-mail messages that Kathryn was receiving on a regular basis now that she had been on the job for awhile. The subject header—"Customer Opportunity Next Week"—seemed innocuous enough, even positive, especially considering that it came from her acerbic chief engineer, Martin. And the note itself was short. The most damaging ones usually are.

That it was not addressed to anyone in particular, but was sent to the entire executive staff, only belied its incendiary potential:

> Just received a call from ASA Manufacturing. They're interested in reviewing our product to consider a purchase next quarter. JR and I will be going down to meet with them next week. Could be a big opportunity. We'll be back early Tuesday.

The fact that Martin avoided any mention of the scheduling conflict with the executive retreat only made the situation worse for Kathryn. He had not asked permission to miss the first day and a half of the off-site retreat, either because he didn't feel the need to do so or because he wanted to avoid having to deal with the issue altogether. Kathryn decided it didn't matter which was true.

She resisted the temptation to avoid a confrontation with Martin by firing off an e-mail reply. Kathryn decided that this would be her first moment of truth as a CEO, and moments of truth, she knew, are best handled face-to-face.

Kathryn found Martin sitting in his corner office reading e-mail. His back was turned toward the open door, but she didn't bother knocking.

"Excuse me, Martin." Kathryn waited for Martin to turn around, which he took his time doing. "I just saw your e-mail about ASA."

He nodded, and she went on. "That's great news. But we'll have to push the appointment back a few days because of the off-site."

Martin was silent for an awkward moment, then responded without emotion but with his thickest English accent. "I don't think you understand. This is a potential sales opportunity. You don't just reschedule . . ."

Kathryn interrupted and responded matter-of-factly. "No, I *do* understand. But I think they'll still be there next week."

Not used to being countered directly, Martin became just slightly agitated. "If your concern is about this Napa off-site thing, then I think we may have our priorities confused. We need to be out there selling."

Kathryn took a breath and smiled to conceal her frustrations. "First of all, I only have one priority at this point: we need to get our act together as a team, or we're not going to be selling anything."

Martin said nothing.

After an awkward five seconds, Kathryn finished the conversation. "So, I'll be seeing you in Napa next week." She turned to leave, then turned back to face Martin again. "Oh, and if you need any help rescheduling the ASA meeting, let me know. I know Bob Tennyson, the CEO down there. He sits on the Trinity board with me, and he owes me a favor."

With that, she left the room. Though Martin decided not to push any further for the moment, he was not through fighting.

END RUN

Jeff stopped by Kathryn's office the next morning and asked her to lunch. She had planned to run an errand during that time, but happily shifted her schedule to accommodate one of her direct reports. The oldest Mexican restaurant in Half Moon Bay was as good a spot as any for a difficult conversation, he thought, because mostly locals ate there.

Before Jeff could broach the topic he wanted to discuss, Kathryn took care of some business of her own. "Jeff, I want to thank you for leading the executive staff meetings these past two weeks. It's allowed me to sit back and observe."

He nodded politely to accept her minor but heartfelt gratitude.

She continued. "After next week's off-site, I'll take over. But I want you to know that you shouldn't hold back during the meetings. You should participate as fully as any other staff member."

Jeff nodded, "Fine. I don't think that will be a problem." He paused, then worked up the courage to raise the issue that had provoked the lunch invitation. Straightening his silverware nervously, he began. "Now that you mention the off-site, I'd like to ask you a question."

"Go ahead." Kathryn was almost amused by Jeff's discomfort. And because she had anticipated a question about her run-in with Martin, she was calm and confident.

"Well, yesterday, on the way out of the office, I talked to Martin in the parking lot." He waited, hoping Kathryn would jump in and move the conversation forward from there. She didn't, so Jeff continued. "Well, he said something to me about the ASA meeting and the off-site scheduling problem."

Again Jeff paused, hoping for his new boss to mercifully interrupt. This time she did, but only to prompt him to continue. "Yes?"

Jeff swallowed. "Well, he believes, and frankly I think I agree with him, that a customer meeting is more important than an internal one. And so, if he and JR missed the first day or so of the off-site, I think we would be okay."

Kathryn chose her words carefully. "Jeff, I understand your opinion, and I'm fine with your disagreeing with me, especially when you tell me face-to-face."

Jeff was noticeably relieved, for the moment.

"However, I was hired to make this organization work, and right now it doesn't."

Jeff looked like he was trying to decide whether to be humbled or angry, so Kathryn clarified. "I'm not trying to criticize what you've done so far, because it seems to me that no one cares more about the company than you do." His ego now assuaged, Kathryn drove the point home. "But from a team standpoint, we are completely broken. And one sales meeting is not going to have a meaningful impact on our future, at least not until we straighten out the leadership problems around here."

Not knowing Kathryn very well, Jeff decided that any further debate would be fruitless and possibly career-limiting. He nodded as if to say, *Okay, I guess it's your call.* The two of them then engaged in small talk and ate one of the fastest lunches in Half Moon Bay history before heading back to the office.

DRAWING THE LINE

The conversation with Jeff had not fazed Kathryn. She had certainly expected some backlash about the Martin incident from her inherited staff. But she didn't expect it to come from the Chairman.

When he reached her at home that evening, she initially assumed he was calling to give her support.

"I just got off the phone with Jeff," he announced in a friendly tone.

"So, I guess you heard about my head-butt with Martin."

Kathryn's humorous and confident attitude pushed the Chairman into a more serious mood. "Yes, and I'm a little concerned."

Kathryn was caught off guard. "You are?"

"Look, Kathryn, you know I don't want to tell you how to go about doing this, but maybe you should try to build a few bridges over there before you start setting any on fire."

Kathryn let a few moments pass before replying. As surprised as she was by the Chairman's concerns, she was remarkably calm and shifted into CEO mode immediately. "Okay, what I'm about to say is not meant in any way to be defensive or rude."

"I know that, Kathryn."

"Good, because I'm not going to mince my words—not with you."

"And I appreciate that."

"You may not after you hear what I have to say."

He forced a laugh. "Okay, I'm sitting down."

"First, don't think that I'm just randomly setting fires to get my kicks. I've been watching these people carefully for the past two weeks, and everything I'm doing, and everything I'm about to do, is purposeful and intentional. I didn't tweak Martin because I felt like it in the moment."

"I know, it's just that . . ."

Kathryn interrupted politely. "Hear me out. This is important."

"Okay, go ahead."

"Now, if you knew how to do what I am trying to do, you wouldn't need me. Am I right?"

"You're right."

"You see, I honestly appreciate your concern for the company, and for me, and I know you mean well on both counts. But based on this call, I'd have to say that your good intentions are hurting the company more than helping it."

"I'm sorry, but I'm not understanding you."

Kathryn went on. "Well, over the past eighteen months, you've been fairly active with Jeff and the rest of the team, more so than most board chairmen, and you've watched this team spiral further and further into dysfunction and chaos. And now you've asked me to help you pull them out of it. Isn't that what you want?"

"Absolutely. That's exactly what I want."

"Then I have a single question for you: Are you prepared for the consequences of letting me do this right? Now don't answer right away." She caught him just as the words were coming out of his mouth. "Think about it for a second."

She let the question sit there before continuing. "This is not going to be easy. Or pretty. Not for the company. Not for the executives. Not for me. And not for you."

The Chairman remained silent, resisting the temptation to assure her that he was prepared to do whatever she needed.

Kathryn interpreted his silence as permission to continue her pointed lecture. "You've probably heard my husband say that a fractured team is just like a broken arm or leg; fixing it is always painful, and sometimes you have to rebreak it to make it heal correctly. And the rebreak hurts a lot more than the initial break, because you have to do it on purpose."

After another long pause, the Chairman spoke. "Okay, Kathryn, I hear you. Do whatever you have to do. I won't get in the way."

Kathryn could tell that he meant it.

Then he asked, "But I do have one final question: How much of this team are you going to have to rebreak?"

"I should know by the end of the month."

NAPA

K athryn chose the Napa Valley for the off-site because it was close enough to the office to avoid expensive and time-consuming travel, but just far enough to feel out of town. And regardless of how many times people have been there, it always seems to make them slow down a pace or two.

The hotel where the meeting would take place was a small inn located in the town of Yountville. Kathryn liked it because it was reasonably priced during the off-season and had just one large and comfortable conference room. It was on the second floor, had its own balcony, and over-looked acres of vineyards.

The meeting was to start at 9:00 A.M., which meant that most of the team would have to leave their homes fairly early in the morning to arrive on time. By 8:45, everyone had arrived, checked their luggage at the front desk, and was seated at the conference table. Everyone but Martin, that is.

Though no one said anything about him, the way they were checking their watches suggested they were all wondering whether he would be on time. Even Kathryn seemed a bit nervous.

She didn't want the first activity of the meeting to be a reprimand of someone for being late. Then, for a split second, she felt a flash of panic, wondering what she would do if he just didn't show up at all. She couldn't very well fire him for not coming to a meeting, could she? Did she have that kind of political capital with the board? *How valuable is this guy, anyway?*

When Martin came through the door at 8:59, Kathryn breathed an inaudible sigh of relief and chastised herself for worrying so much. She took comfort in knowing that she was finally about to begin what she had been waiting to do for almost a month. And as concerned as she was about the attitudes of the people sitting around the table, Kathryn could not deny that moments like this were a big part of why she loved being a leader.

THE SPEECH

Martin took the only remaining chair at the end of the conference table opposite Kathryn. As soon as he sat down, he removed his laptop computer from its case and put it on the table in front of him, leaving it closed for the moment.

Determined not to be distracted, Kathryn smiled at her staff and addressed them calmly and gracefully.

"Good morning, everyone. I'd like to start the day by saying a few words. And this won't be the last time I say them." No one knew just how serious Kathryn was about that remark.

"We have a more experienced and talented executive team than any of our competitors. We have more cash than they do. Thanks to Martin and his team, we have better core technology. And we have a more powerful board of directors. Yet in spite of all that, we are behind two of our competitors in terms of both revenue and customer growth. Can anyone here tell me why that is?"

Silence.

Kathryn continued, still as warmly as when she started. "After interviewing with every member of our board and spending time with each of you, and then talking to most of our employees, it is very clear to me what our problem is." She paused before completing the thought. "We are not functioning as a team. In fact, we are quite dysfunctional."

A few of the staff members shot glances toward Jeff to see how he would react. He seemed fine, but Kathryn picked up on the tension.

"I'm not saying this to call out Jeff, or anyone else, in particular. It's just a fact. One that we are going to begin addressing over these next two days. And, yes, I know how ridiculous and unbelievable it feels for you to be out of the office for so many days this month. But by the end of it all, everyone who is still here will understand why this is so important."

That last comment got everyone's attention. "That's right. I want to say right up front that DecisionTech is going to experience some changes during the next few months, and it is very possible that some of us here won't find the new company to be the kind of place where we want to be. That isn't a threat or a dramatic device, and I don't have anyone in particular in mind. It's just a realistic probability, and it's nothing to be in denial about. All of us are eminently employable, and it wouldn't be the end of the world for anyone to leave if that is the right thing for the company—and the team."

Kathryn stood and went to the white board, careful not to come across as arrogant or condescending. "Let me assure those of you who might be wondering about all of this that everything we are going to be doing is about one thing only: making this company succeed. That's all. We're not going to be catching each other falling out of trees."

A few of her staff members chuckled.

"And we certainly won't be holding hands, singing songs, or getting naked."

Even Martin managed a smile while the others laughed out loud.

"I want to assure you that there is only one reason that we are here at this off-site, and at the company: to achieve results. This, in my opinion, is the only true measure of a team, and it will be the focus of everything we do today and as long as I'm here. It is my expectation that next year and the year after that, we will be able to look back on revenue growth, profitability, customer retention, and satisfaction, and if the market is right for it, maybe even an IPO. But I can promise you that none of that will happen if we do not address the issues that are preventing us from acting like a team."

Kathryn paused to let everyone digest the simplicity of her message, and then continued. "So how do we go about this? Over the years I've come to the conclusion that there are five reasons why teams are dysfunctional."

She then drew a triangle on the white board and divided it with four horizontal lines, creating five separate sections.

Kathryn then turned back to the group. "Over the course of the next two days, we are going to be filling in this model and dealing with each issue one at a time. And you'll notice immediately that none of this is rocket science. In fact, it will seem remarkably simple on paper. The trick is putting it into practice."

"Right now I'd like to start with the first dysfunction: *absence of trust*." She turned and wrote the phrase at the bottom of the triangle.

The staff members read the words silently, and most of them frowned as if to say, *Is that all you've got?*

Kathryn was used to this and continued. "Trust is the foundation of real teamwork. And so the first dysfunction is a failure on the part of team members to understand and

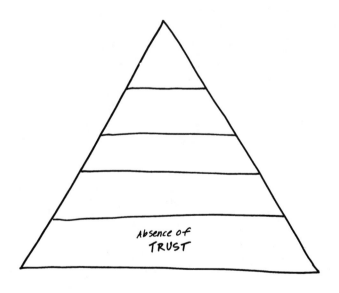

open up to one another. And if that sounds touchy-feely, let me explain, because there is nothing soft about it. It is an absolutely critical part of building a team. In fact, it's probably the most critical."

Some of the people in the room were clearly in need of an explanation.

"Great teams do not hold back with one another," she said. "They are unafraid to air their dirty laundry. They admit their mistakes, their weaknesses, and their concerns without fear of reprisal."

Most of the staff seemed to be accepting the point, but without a lot of enthusiasm.

Kathryn pushed on. "The fact is, if we don't trust one another—and it seems to me that we don't—then we cannot be the kind of team that ultimately achieves results. And so that is where we're going to focus first."

PUSHING BACK

The room was silent, until Jan raised her hand.

Kathryn smiled. "I may have been a school teacher once, but you don't have to raise your hand to talk. Feel free to jump in any time."

Jan nodded and asked her question. "I'm not trying to be negative or contradictory here, but I'm just wondering why you don't think we trust each other. Is it possible that you just don't know us very well yet?"

Kathryn paused to consider the question, wanting to give a thoughtful answer. "Well, my assessment is based on quite a bit of data, Jan. Specific comments from the board, employees, even many of you."

Jan seemed content with the answer, but Kathryn decided to continue. "But I'd have to say that more than anything I've been told by others, I see a trust problem here in the lack of debate that exists during staff meetings and other interactions among this team. But I don't want to get ahead of myself, because that's a separate part of the model entirely."

Nick was not about to let it go. "But that doesn't always mean there is an absence of trust, does it?" The question was more of a statement than anything else. Everyone in the room, including Martin and Mikey, seemed eager for Kathryn's response.

"No, not necessarily, I guess."

Nick was momentarily pleased that his comment was deemed to be correct.

Until Kathryn clarified. "Theoretically, if everyone is completely on the same page and working in lockstep toward the same goals with no sense of confusion, then I suppose a lack of debate might be a good sign."

More than one of the staff members began to smile sheepishly at the description that certainly did not apply to them. Nick's satisfaction disappeared.

Kathryn continued to direct her explanation toward him. "But I'd have to say that every effective team I've ever observed had a substantial level of debate. Even the most trusting teams mixed it up a lot." Now she directed a question to the rest of the room. "Why do you suppose there is so little passionate discussion or debate among this group?"

At first no one answered, and Kathryn let them sit in the uncomfortable silence. Then Mikey mumbled something under her breath.

"I'm sorry, Mikey. I didn't hear you." Kathryn did her best to conceal her distaste for sarcastic remarks, which she had developed teaching seventh graders.

Mikey clarified, louder now. "There isn't enough time. I think we're all too busy to have lengthy debates about minor issues. We're drowning in work as it is."

Kathryn sensed that the others might not agree with Mikey, but she wondered if anyone dared challenge her. She was about to do so herself, when Jeff offered tentatively, "I'm not sure I'm with you on that one, Mikey. I don't think we lack the time to argue. I think we're just not comfortable challenging each other. And I'm not sure why."

Mikey responded quickly, if not sharply. "Maybe because our meetings are always too structured and boring."

The mother in Kathryn wanted to step in and protect Jeff, partly to reward him for having stood up to Mikey. But she decided to let things go.

After a pause, Carlos chimed in gently, but without directing his comments at Mikey, as though the entire group had made the remark. "Now wait a minute, everyone. I agree that meetings have been pretty dull and that the agenda is usually a little too full. But I think we all could have challenged each other more. We certainly don't all agree on everything."

Nick spoke up. "I don't think we agree on anything."

They all laughed—except Martin, who had opened his laptop and turned it on.

Kathryn joined the livening conversation. "So you don't agree on most things, and yet you don't seem willing to admit that you have concerns. Now, I'm no Ph.D.

in psychology, but that's a trust issue if I've ever heard one." A few of the heads in the room actually nodded in agreement with Kathryn, something she appreciated like a starving person given a few morsels of bread.

And then the typing sound began. Martin, now completely checked out of the conversation, was banging away at his keyboard like, well, like a computer programmer. Distracted by the sound, everyone in the room glanced at Martin for a nanosecond. And that was enough to kill whatever momentum the conversation had generated.

Kathryn had both relished this moment and dreaded it from the first staff meeting she had observed. And as much as she wanted to avoid another run-in with Martin, especially so early in the day, she would not let the opportunity pass her by.

ENTERING
THE DANGER

The tension in the room began to mount as Kathryn watched Martin type away at the other end of the table. No one really thought she would say anything. But they didn't know Kathryn very well.

"Excuse me, Martin."

Martin finished typing and then looked up to acknowledge his boss.

"Are you working on something?" Kathryn's question was sincere, without even a hint of sarcasm.

The room froze, waiting anxiously for the answer to the question they had been wanting to ask for the past two years.

Martin seemed as though he wasn't going to respond at all, then said, "I'm taking notes, actually," and continued typing.

Kathryn remained calm and continued to speak in a measured tone. "I think this is a good time to talk about ground rules for the off-site and for our meetings going forward."

Martin looked up from his computer, and Kathryn continued, directing her comments to the entire group. "I don't have a lot of rules when it comes to meetings. But there are a few that I'm a stickler about."

Everyone waited for her to begin.

"Basically, I want you all to do two things: be present and participate. That means everyone needs to be fully engaged in whatever we're talking about."

Even Martin knew when to pull back a little. He asked a question, but in a slightly conciliatory tone that the group was not accustomed to hearing from their chief scientist. "What about when the conversation is not relevant to everyone? Sometimes it seems that we talk about issues that would best be handled off-line. One-on-one."

"That's a good point." Kathryn was reeling Martin in now. "If there is ever a time when that happens, when we think that we're wasting the group's time by dealing with issues that should be dealt with outside the meeting, then everyone here should feel free to speak up."

Martin seemed pleased that she had agreed with him.

Kathryn went on. "But for everything else, I want everyone fully engaged. And while I understand that some people prefer to use a computer rather than a notebook, like you, Martin, I've found that it's just too distracting. It's easy to imagine the person sitting there checking e-mail or working on something else."

Mikey decided to come to Martin's aid, something he didn't want or need. "Kathryn, with all due respect, you haven't worked within the high-tech culture, and this is pretty common in software companies. I mean, maybe not in the automotive world, but . . ."

Kathryn interrupted politely. "Actually, this is very common in the automotive world. I had the same issue there. It's more of a behavioral issue than a technological one."

Jeff nodded and smiled as if to say, *Good answer.* And with that, Martin closed his laptop and put it in his computer case. More than one of the staff members looked at Kathryn as if she had just talked a bank robber into handing over his gun.

If only the rest of the day would be so easy.

GETTING NAKED

Kathryn knew that she was about to begin a deceptively critical part of the session, one that would give her clues as to how things might unfold during the months ahead. It was no accident that it was the first real exercise on the agenda.

"Before we get into any heavy lifting, let's start with something that I call personal histories."

Kathryn explained that everyone would answer five nonintrusive personal questions having to do with their backgrounds, and she ended her instructions with a humorous caveat that even Martin seemed to appreciate. "Remember, I want to hear about your life as a child, but I'm not interested in your inner child."

One by one the DecisionTech executives answered the questions. Hometown? Number of kids in the family? Interesting childhood hobbies? Biggest challenge growing up? First job?

Almost to a person, every set of answers contained a gem or two that few, if any, of the other executives knew.

Carlos was the oldest of nine kids. Mikey studied ballet at the Juilliard School in New York. Jeff had been a batboy for the Boston Red Sox. Martin spent much of his childhood in India. JR has an identical twin brother. Jan was a military brat. During the discussion, Nick even discovered that he had played basketball in high school against the team coached by Kathryn's husband.

As for Kathryn, her staff seemed most surprised and impressed not by her military training or automotive experience, but by the fact that she had been an All-American volleyball player in college.

It was really quite amazing. After just forty-five minutes of extremely mild personal disclosure, the team seemed tighter and more at ease with each other than at any time during the past year. But Kathryn had been through this enough to know that the euphoria would diminish as soon as the conversation shifted to work.

GOING DEEPER

When the team returned from a short break, it was clear that they had already lost some of the glow from the morning's session. They spent the next several hours, working through lunch, reviewing their individual behavioral tendencies according to a variety of diagnostic tools that they had completed before coming to Napa. One of these was the Myers-Briggs Type Indicator.

Kathryn was pleasantly surprised that even Martin seemed to be engaged in the discussion. But then again, she reasoned, everyone likes to learn about—and talk about—themselves. Until the criticism comes, that is. And it was about to come.

But Kathryn decided that late afternoon was a bad time to dive into the next phase, given everyone's energy level. So she gave them a break for a few hours in the afternoon, to check e-mail, exercise, or do whatever else they wanted. Kathryn knew they would be working late that night, and she didn't want them to get burned out too early.

Martin spent most of the afternoon break reading e-mail in his room. Nick, Jeff, Carlos, and JR played bocce ball on the court next to the hotel, and Kathryn and Jan met in the lobby to talk about budgets. Mikey sat by the pool and read a novel.

When they returned around dinnertime, Kathryn was pleased to see them pick up the conversation where it had ended earlier. By now, everyone had acknowledged their different interpersonal styles at work and discussed the implications of being an introvert versus an extrovert and other similar qualities. They all were definitely loosening up.

People were eating pizza and beer, which made everything seem less threatening. Suddenly, Carlos was teasing Jan for being too anal, while Jeff razzed JR for being unfocused. Even Martin responded well when Nick called him a "raging introvert." No one at the table was fazed by the good-natured but substantive ribbing, with the exception of Mikey. It wasn't that she took their teasing badly. Worse yet, no one teased her at all. In fact, they made no comments about her, and unsurprisingly, she made almost none about them.

Kathryn wanted to bring her into the process but decided not to be too aggressive so soon. Things were going well—better than she had expected—and the team seemed willing to talk about some of the dysfunctional behaviors that Kathryn had observed during staff meetings. There was no need to create a controversy on the first night, especially after already having dodged a few bullets with Martin.

But sometimes things cannot be controlled, and Mikey herself opened up the door to her own issues. When Nick remarked to the group that he found the personality descriptions to be amazingly accurate and helpful, Mikey did what she so often did during staff meetings: she rolled her eyes.

Kathryn was just about to call her on her behavior, when Nick beat her to it. "What was that all about?"

Mikey reacted as though she had no idea what he was referring to. "What?"

Nick was mostly teasing her, but he was clearly a little annoyed. "Come on. You rolled your eyes. Did I say something stupid?"

She persisted in feigning ignorance. "No, I didn't say anything."

Now Jan jumped in, but gently. "You didn't have to say anything, Mikey. It was the look on your face." Jan wanted to defuse the situation by helping Mikey 'fess up without losing face. "Sometimes I think that you don't even know you're doing it."

But Mikey wouldn't bite, and she was beginning to get ever so slightly defensive. "I really don't know what you're talking about."

Nick couldn't hold back. "Come on. You do it all the time. It's like you think we're all idiots."

Kathryn made a mental note not to have beer brought with dinner next time. But she couldn't deny being glad that things were coming to the surface. She took a bite of pizza and watched with everyone else, resisting the temptation to make artificial peace.

Out of nowhere, Mikey responded. "Listen, you guys. I'm not into all this psychobabble. I don't think any of our competitors, who happen to be kicking our asses right now, are sitting around a hotel in Napa talking about where they get their energy or how they see the world."

The room was caught off guard by the indictment of the entire process, which they seemed to be enjoying, and looked to Kathryn to see how she would respond. But Martin beat her to it.

"Yeah, you're right." People were shocked that Martin, who seemed engaged in the process, was defending Mikey—until he completed the punch line of his remark. "They're probably in Carmel."

Had anyone else said it, the room would have chuckled. But coming from Martin and directed at Mikey in his dry, sarcastic accent, it made everyone howl. Except, of course, Mikey, who just sat there smiling painfully.

For a moment Kathryn thought her marketing VP would walk out. That might have been better than what she did. For the next ninety minutes, Mikey didn't say a word, but sat silently as the group continued their discussion.

Eventually, the topic naturally drifted toward more tactical topics related to the business. Jan interrupted the conversation and asked Kathryn, "Are we getting off track here?"

Kathryn shook her head. "No, I think it's good that we dive into operational issues while we're talking about behavioral stuff. It gives us a chance to see how we put this into action."

As happy as Kathryn was by the interaction that was taking place among the rest of the team, she couldn't overlook the fact that Mikey's behavior was speaking volumes about her inability to trust her teammates.

POOLSIDE

Kathryn called the session to an end a little after 10:00 P.M., and with the exception of Jan and Nick who had just begun an impromptu budget discussion, the team headed to bed. Mikey and Kathryn's rooms were near the pool at the small hotel complex, and as they walked to their rooms, Kathryn decided to see if she could make some progress one-on-one.

"You okay?" Kathryn was careful not to be too dramatic or maternal.

"I'm fine." Mikey wasn't faking very well.

"I know this is a difficult process, and that you might feel like they were a little tough on you."

"A little? Listen, I don't let people make fun of me at home, and I sure as hell don't want people to do it at work. Those guys have no idea about how to make a company successful."

Kathryn was almost too confused by the scattershot reply to respond. After a few moments, she said, "Well, we can talk about that tomorrow. I think they need to hear what you think."

"Oh, I'm not saying anything tomorrow."

Kathryn tried not to overreact to Mikey's comment, which she attributed more to her momentary emotions than anything else. "I think you'll feel better in the morning."

"No, I'm serious. They aren't going to hear from me."

Kathryn decided to let it go for the moment. "Well, get a good night's sleep."

They were at their rooms now. Mikey ended the conversation with a sarcastic laugh. "Oh, I will."

REBOUND

Only Kathryn and Jan were in the conference room when Mikey arrived the next morning. She seemed enthusiastic and unbowed by the previous day's events, which was a pleasant surprise for Kathryn.

Once the others had arrived, Kathryn kicked off the session with an abbreviated version of the prior day's speech. "Okay, before we get started, I think it's good to remember why we are here. We have more cash, more experienced executives, better technology, and more connections than any of our competitors, and yet at least two of them are ahead of us in the market. Our job is to increase revenue, profitability, and customer acquisition and retention and maybe even put ourselves in a position for an IPO. But none of this will happen if we don't function as a team."

She paused, surprised at how closely her reports seemed to be listening. It was as if they were hearing it for the first time. "Any questions?"

Instead of just sitting there silently, a number of the staff members shook their heads as if to say, *No questions; let's get started.* At least that's how Kathryn interpreted it.

For the next few hours, the group reviewed the material they had covered the previous day. After an hour or so, Martin and Nick seemed to be losing a little interest, and JR became more distracted each time his cell phone vibrated and went unanswered.

Kathryn decided to address their concerns before they started talking among themselves. "I know that you're all probably starting to wonder, 'Didn't we do this yesterday?' And I realize it's repetitive. But this stuff won't stick unless we understand how to apply it completely."

For another hour, the group discussed the implications of their various style preferences and the collective opportunities and challenges that those styles created. Mikey made few comments, and whenever she did speak, the flow of conversation seemed to slow dramatically. Martin too said little, but seemed to be paying attention and following the conversation nonetheless.

By midmorning, they had completed their review of interpersonal styles and team behaviors. And then, with less than an hour until lunch, Kathryn decided to introduce the most important exercise of the day, one that she would look back on later as a moment of truth for Mikey and the rest of the team.

AWARENESS

Walking back to the white board, Kathryn explained, "Remember, teamwork begins by building trust. And the only way to do that is to overcome our need for invulnerability." She wrote the word *invulnerability* next to *trust* on the white board.

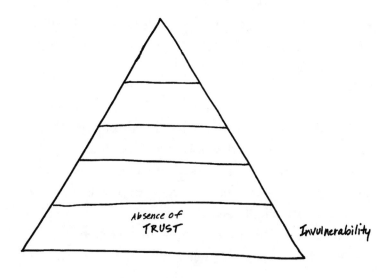

Then she continued. "And so, we are all going to demonstrate vulnerability this morning in a low-risk but relevant way."

She then asked everyone to spend five minutes deciding what they believed were their single biggest strength and weakness in terms of their contribution to Decision-Tech's success or failure. "I don't want you to give me some generic weakness, and I don't want you glossing over your strengths because you're too modest or embarrassed to tell us what you think you're really good at. Take this simple exercise seriously, and be willing to put yourself out there."

When it was clear that everyone had finished jotting down their notes, Kathryn began the discussion. "Okay, I'll go first." She looked at her notes briefly. "I think my biggest strength, at least the strength that will have the biggest impact on our success, is my ability to see through fluffy, superfluous information and cut to the point that matters. I have a way of eliminating unnecessary details and getting to the heart of an issue, and that should save us a lot of time."

She paused before continuing. "My weakness is that I am not the world's best external spokesperson. In fact, I'm bad at it. I tend to downplay the importance of public relations, and I'm not a talented or tactful speaker when it comes to being in front of a large group or, even worse, a television camera. I'm going to need help with that if we are going to accomplish everything that we hope to."

With the exception of JR and Mikey, everyone was taking notes as Kathryn spoke. She liked that. "Okay, who wants to go next?"

No one volunteered immediately. Everyone was looking around—some hoping that one of their peers would volunteer, others seeming to ask permission to step forward.

Finally, Nick broke the ice. "I'll go. Okay, let's see." He reviewed his notes. "My biggest strength is my lack of fear when it comes to negotiation and management of outside companies, whether they're partners, vendors, or competitors. I don't have any problem pushing them to do more than they want to do. My biggest weakness, however, is that I sometimes come across as arrogant."

A few of Nick's peers laughed a little nervously.

He smiled and continued. "Yes, I've had that problem since I was in college, and probably before. I can be sarcastic and even rude at times, and sometimes I come across sounding like I think I'm smarter than everyone else. And that might be okay, I suppose, if I'm dealing with a vendor, but with you guys, it could probably piss you off a little, which I don't think is going to help us get where we want to go."

Jeff commented, "It sounds like your strength and weakness are rooted in the same things."

Martin, to everyone's surprise, voiced his agreement. "Isn't that usually the case?"

Heads around the table nodded.

Kathryn was impressed by the apparent honesty of Nick's remarks and the willingness of the other staff members to make comments. She was glad he went first. "Good. That was exactly the kind of thing I'm looking for. Who's next?"

Jan volunteered and talked about her management skills and attention to detail as strengths, something everyone agreed with immediately. Then she admitted being more conservative about finances than the CFO of a start-up should be. She explained that this was a result of her training at larger companies and her concern that her peers were not concerned enough about managing expenses. "Still, I am probably making it harder for you all to meet me halfway by being so controlling."

Carlos assured her that the rest of the group could probably take a step or two in her direction.

Jeff went next. He struggled in his attempt to call out his amazing networking skills and ability to build partnerships with investors and partners.

But Jan wouldn't let him off the hook. "Come on now, Jeff. If we've done one thing well, it's been raising boatloads of money and getting investors excited about the company. Don't downplay your role in that."

Jeff reluctantly accepted her kind-hearted rebuke, and then blew everyone away with his admission of weakness. "I am pretty afraid to fail. And so I tend to over-engineer things and do them myself. I don't like to tell other people what to do, which, ironically, only makes it more likely that I'm going to fail."

For the slightest moment, Jeff seemed to fight back emotions and then recovered instantly. He was sure no one noticed. "And I think that's probably the biggest reason that we haven't succeeded, and that I'm not the CEO anymore." He paused, and then added quickly, "Which I'm okay with, really. In fact, I'm pretty happy to be out of that job."

The group laughed in a supportive way.

Kathryn couldn't believe that the first three people to step forward had done so well. For a moment, she began to entertain hopes that the momentum would continue and the day would be a runaway hit. And then Mikey spoke.

"Okay, I'll go next." Unlike her peers who had gone before her, Mikey looked at her notes almost the entire time that she talked. "My biggest strength is my understanding of the technology market and how to communicate with analysts and the media. My biggest weakness is my poor financial skills."

Silence. No comments. No questions. Nothing.

Like Kathryn, most everyone in the room was torn between two emotions: relief that Mikey was finished, and disappointment at the shallow nature of her response. At that moment, Kathryn didn't feel that it would be right to force her vice president of marketing to be more vulnerable. Mikey had to do it herself.

With every second that went by, the group quietly begged for someone to break the silence. Carlos put them out of their misery.

"Okay, I'll go next." Doing his best to bring the quality of the conversation back to a higher level, he talked about his follow-through as a strength and his failure to update people on his progress as a weakness.

After he finished, Jan jumped in. "Carlos, I think you missed on both of your answers." Kathryn, not knowing that Carlos and Jan had become fairly close, was surprised by the directness of her remark.

Jan continued. "First, as thorough as you are, your willingness to do the shit work and not complain is your strength. I know that sounds terrible, but I don't know what would happen around here if you weren't bailing us out all the time." A number of the others voiced their agreement. "And on the negative side, I think you could tell us what you're thinking more during meetings. You hold back too much."

Everyone seemed to wait to see how Carlos would respond, but he just nodded his head and took a note. "Okay."

JR volunteered to go next and brought the room to a roar when he explained, "Clearly, my biggest strength is my follow-through and attention to detail." The group enjoyed the laughter for a few minutes, until JR continued. "Seriously, I'm pretty good at building strong personal relationships with customers. In fact, I'm really good at that." He said it modestly enough for everyone to appreciate. "On the downside, if I don't think something is terribly important, which usually means it isn't going to get me closer to closing a deal, I can sometimes blow it off."

"Sometimes?" asked Nick. The room howled again.

JR blushed. "I know, I know. I just can't seem to get around to my to-do list. I don't know why. But I think that hurts the team."

Martin was the only remaining executive. "Okay, I think I'm next." He took a deep breath. "I hate talking about myself this way, but if I have to, I'd say that I'm good at solving problems, doing analysis—stuff like that. What I'm not so good at is communicating with human beings." He stopped. "I mean, it's not that I can't do it, but I really prefer people who aren't sensitive. I like to have conversations with people on a purely intellectual level and not have to worry about what they're feeling or anything like that. Does that make sense?"

"Sure," said Jeff, who decided to take a risk. "The problem is that it can sometimes make people think you don't like them. That they're a waste of your time."

Martin seemed visibly disappointed by Jeff's remark. "No, that's not it at all. I mean, that's not what I intend. Crap. That's bad. I don't mean that at all, but I suppose I can see how it comes across that way. I don't know how to change that."

For the first time all morning, Mikey chimed in, smiling. "Years of psychotherapy, my friend. And even then, you probably wouldn't be able to change it. You're just an arrogant s.o.b. But then again, isn't every CTO in the Valley?"

Mikey laughed. No one else did, with the exception of Martin, who seemed embarrassed by her remark and wanted to add to its sense of being humorous. Inside, he was melting.

Kathryn would later kick herself for not calling Mikey on her remark, which at the time Kathryn attributed to her astonishingly low emotional intelligence. Whatever the case, it was clear to her now that Mikey's behavior was having a very real impact on the rest of the group.

EGO

Whitten everyone had found their seats around the table, Kathryn announced the change in direction. "Okay, we're going to move all the way to the final dysfunction, but we'll be revisiting the fear-of-vulnerability topic and the need for trust many, many times again over the course of the next month. If anyone isn't looking forward to that, you'd better brace yourself."

Everyone assumed she was talking to Mikey. None of them could have guessed that another member of the team was struggling as much as she was.

Kathryn described the next dysfunction by going to the white board and writing the phrase *inattention to results* at the top of the triangle.

"We are going to the top of the chart now to talk about the ultimate dysfunction: the tendency of team members to seek out individual recognition and attention at the expense of results. And I'm referring to collective results—the goals of the entire team."

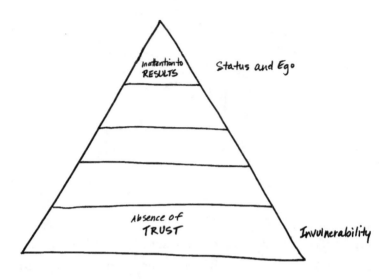

Nick asked, "Is this about ego?"

"Well, I suppose that's part of it," agreed Kathryn. "But I'm not saying that there's no place for ego on a team. The key is to make the collective ego greater than the individual ones."

"I'm not sure I understand what this has to do with results," Jeff remarked.

"Well, when everyone is focused on results and using those to define success, it is difficult for ego to get out of hand. No matter how good an individual on the team might be feeling about his or her situation, if the team loses, everyone loses."

Kathryn could see that a few of her reports were not quite with her yet, so she took another approach. "I told you yesterday that my husband is a basketball coach at St. Jude's High School in San Mateo."

"He's a damn good basketball coach," explained Nick. "He's been getting job offers from colleges since I was in high school, and every year he turns them down. He's a legend."

Kathryn was proud of her husband and enjoyed Nick's commentary. "Yeah, I suppose he is something of an anomaly, and he's certainly good at what he does. Anyway, he is all about the team. And as good as his teams are, few of his kids play ball at big colleges because, frankly, they're not all that talented. They win because they play team basketball, and that usually allows them to beat bigger, faster, more talented groups of players."

Nick was nodding his head with the certainty of someone who had lost to St. Jude's many times.

"Well, every once in a while, Ken, that's my husband, gets a player on his team who doesn't really care about results. Or at least not the results of the team. I remember a kid a few years ago who was interested only in his own statistics and whether he received individual recognition: All-League, picture in the paper, that sort of stuff. If the team lost, he would be in a good mood as long as he was getting his points. And even when the team won, he would be unhappy if he didn't score enough."

Jan was curious. "What did your husband do about him?"

Kathryn smiled, eager to tell them more about Ken. "That's the interesting thing. This kid was without a doubt one of the most talented players on the team. But Ken benched him. The team played better without him, and he eventually quit."

"Harsh," remarked JR.

"Yeah, but he came out the next year with a very different attitude, and went on to play for Saint Mary's College after he graduated. He'll tell you now that it was the most important year of his life."

Jan was still curious. "Do you think most people like that can change?"

Kathryn didn't hesitate. "No. For every kid like that one, there are ten who never made it." The group seemed sobered by the definitive response, and more than one of them were thinking about Mikey at that moment. "And as harsh as that may sound, Ken always says that his job is to create the best team possible, not to shepherd the careers of individual athletes. And that's how I look at my job."

Jeff decided to ask the group a question. "Anyone here play team sports in high school or college?"

Kathryn wanted to stop Jeff's poll and keep the discussion moving in the direction she had planned. But she decided that a little impromptu discussion was probably as valuable for the team as anything else, as long as it had something to do with teamwork.

Jeff went around the room, giving every person a chance to respond to his question.

Nick reported that he had played baseball in college. Carlos was a linebacker in high school.

Martin proudly announced, "I played football, the original kind." Everyone chuckled at their European colleague.

Mikey said she ran track in high school.

When Nick questioned her, "But that's an individual . . . ," she interrupted him cleverly, "I ran on the relay team."

Kathryn reminded everyone that she was a volleyball player.

Jan reported that she was a cheerleader and a member of the dance team. "And if anyone here says those aren't teams, I'm going to cut your budget in half."

They laughed.

Jeff confessed his lack of athletic aptitude. "You see, I don't understand why everyone thinks sports is the only way to learn about teamwork. I never played sports much, even as a kid. But I was in a band in high school and college, and I think I figured out the team thing from that."

Kathryn saw an opportunity to regain control of the discussion. "Aha. That's a good point. First of all, you can definitely learn teamwork from lots of different activities, pretty much anything that involves a group of people working together. But there is a reason that sports are so prevalent when it comes to teams." The seventh-grade teacher in Kathryn suddenly emerged, wanting to give her pupils a chance to answer her next question themselves. "Does anyone know what that is?"

Like so many times in her classroom, the group seemed to have no clue. But Kathryn knew that if she could tolerate the silence for a moment, soon enough someone would come up with the answer. This time it was Martin.

"The score." As usual, Martin provided little context for his answer.

"Explain," commanded Kathryn, just as she would have done with one of her students.

"Well, in most sports, there is a clear score at the end of the game that determines whether you succeeded or failed. There is little room for ambiguity, which means there is little room for . . ." He paused to find the right words. ". . . for subjective, interpretive, ego-driven success, if you know what I mean."

Heads around the room nodded to say that everyone did.

"Wait a second," demanded JR. "Are you telling me that athletes don't have egos?"

Martin seemed at a loss, so Kathryn jumped in. "They have huge egos. But great athletes' egos are usually tied to a clear result: winning. They just want to win. More than making the All-Star team, more than getting their picture on a box of Wheaties, and yes, more than making money."

"I'm not sure there are many of those kinds of teams around anymore, at least not in professional sports," declared Nick.

Kathryn smiled. "And that's the beauty. The teams that figure it out have a bigger advantage than ever before because most of their competitors are just a bunch of individuals looking out for themselves."

Mikey was looking a little bored. "What does this have to do with a software company?"

Again, Mikey brought the conversation to a halt. But Kathryn wanted to encourage her in any way she could, though she was already starting to doubt the likelihood of turning her around. "Another good question. This has everything to do with us. You see, we are going to make our collective results as important as the score at a football game. We aren't going to leave any room for interpretation when it comes to our success, because that only creates the opportunity for individual ego to sneak in."

"Don't we already have a scoreboard?" Mikey persisted.

"You're talking about profit?" asked Kathryn.

Mikey nodded and made a face as if to say, *What else?*

Kathryn continued, patiently. "Certainly profit is a big part of it. But I'm talking more about near-term results. If you let profit be your only guide to results, you won't be able to know how the team is doing until the season is almost over."

"Now I'm confused," admitted Carlos. "Isn't profit the only score that matters?"

Kathryn smiled. "Yeah, I'm starting to get a little too academic here. So let me make this simple. Our job is to make the results that we need to achieve so clear to everyone in this room that no one would even consider doing something purely to enhance his or her individual status or ego. Because that would diminish our ability to achieve our collective goals. We would all lose."

Something seemed to be catching on just slightly, so Kathryn pushed forward. "The key, of course, is to define our goals, our results, in a way that is simple enough to grasp easily, and specific enough to be actionable. Profit is not actionable enough. It needs to be more closely related to what we do on a daily basis. And to that end, let's see if we can come up with something right now."

GOALS

Kathryn then broke everyone into groups of two or three and asked each group to propose a list of results categories that might serve as the team's scoreboard. "Don't quantify any of this yet; just create the categories."

Within the hour, the group had generated more than fifteen different kinds of results categories. By combining some and eliminating others, they narrowed them to seven: revenue, expenses, new customer acquisition, current customer satisfaction, employee retention, market awareness, and product quality. They also decided that these should be measured monthly, because waiting a full quarter to track results didn't give them enough opportunities to detect problems and alter activities sufficiently.

Unfortunately, now that the discussion was turning back toward the business, some of the levity in the room seemed to evaporate. As usual, it would be replaced by criticism.

Martin began. "I'm sorry, but this is nothing new, Kathryn. Those are pretty much the same metrics that we've been using for the past nine months."

It felt as if part of Kathryn's credibility was diminishing right before their eyes.

JR piled on. "Yeah, and none of it has helped us drive revenue. Frankly, I'm not sure any of these matter if we don't get a few deals closed, and fast."

Kathryn was almost amused at the predictability of what was unfolding before her. As soon as the reality of business problems is reintroduced to a situation like this one, she thought, people revert back to the behaviors that put them in the difficult situation in the first place. But she was ready.

"Okay, Martin. Can you tell me what our market awareness goal for last quarter was?"

Mikey corrected her boss. "We call it public relations activity."

"Okay, fine." She turned back to Martin. "Can you tell me exactly what the PR goal was?"

"No. But I'm sure that Mikey can. I can tell you what our product development dates are, though."

"Okay. Then just tell me how we did in terms of public relations activity?" She directed the question at Martin again, making it clear that he ought to know the answer.

He seemed puzzled. "Hell, I don't know. I assume that Jeff and Mikey talk about that stuff. But I'm also assuming that we didn't do very well, given our sales numbers."

Mikey was remarkably calm, which only made her subsequent remarks all the more unpleasant. "Listen, I came to the meetings every week with my PR numbers, but no one ever asked about them. And besides, I can't get us any press if we don't sell anything."

Though JR should have been more upset than anyone by the remark, Martin was the one to respond. And he did so sarcastically. "That's funny. I always thought that the purpose of marketing was to drive sales. I guess I've had that backward."

Almost as though she hadn't heard Martin's remark, Mikey continued to defend herself. "I can tell you that the problems we're having are not due to marketing. In fact, I think my department has done remarkably well given what we've had to work with."

Carlos wanted to say *but your department cannot be doing well because the company is failing and if the company is failing then we are all failing and there is no way that we can justify the performance of our own departments* . . . But he didn't want to push Mikey any harder, sensing that his colleague might snap under the pressure, and so he let it go.

As frustrated as everyone was at that moment, Kathryn was sure that a much-needed melee was about to ensue. But just like that, the conversation came to a halt. And died.

So this is how it works, she thought to herself.

DEEP TISSUE

Kathryn was determined not to lose the momentum.

"Okay, I think I see the underlying problem."

Jeff smiled and responded sarcastically, but in a nice way. "Really?"

Kathryn laughed. "Pretty observant of me, huh? Anyway, when I talk about focusing on results instead of individual recognition, I'm talking about everyone adopting a set of common goals and measurements, and then actually using them to make collective decisions on a daily basis."

Seeing that they weren't going to cede the obvious point easily, Kathryn decided to shift back toward a more questioning approach. "How often did you all talk about moving resources from one department to another in the middle of the quarter in order to make sure that you could achieve a goal that was in jeopardy?"

The looks on their faces said *Never*.

"And how disciplined were you during meetings about reviewing the goals in detail and drilling down on why they were or weren't being met?" She already knew the answer.

Jeff explained. "I have to say that I just considered it Mikey's job to do marketing, Martin's to develop products, JR's to make sales. I would pitch in whenever I could, but otherwise, I let them be accountable for their own areas. And I dealt with their issues on a one-on-one basis whenever I could."

Kathryn went back to the sports analogy, hoping this would get through to them. "Okay, imagine a basketball coach in the locker room at half-time. He calls the team's center into his office to talk with him one-on-one about the first half, and then he does the same with the point guard, the shooting guard, the small forward, and the power forward, without any of them knowing what everyone else was talking about. That's not a team. It's a collection of individuals."

And it was clear to everyone in the room that this was exactly what the DecisionTech executive staff was.

Kathryn was smiling in disbelief, as if to say, *I can't believe that I have to tell you this.* In a more patient tone, she said, "All of you, every one of you, are responsible for sales. Not just JR. All of you are responsible for marketing. Not just Mikey. All of you are responsible for product development, customer service, and finance. Does that make sense?"

Confronted by the simplicity and truth of Kathryn's plea, and their obvious inadequacies as a group, any illusions of unity that had survived the first day and a half now appeared to be gone.

Nick was shaking his head and then spoke, as if he couldn't hold back any longer. "You know, I just wonder whether we have the right people sitting at this table. Maybe we need more heavy hitters who can get us into the right accounts, and develop the right strategic partnerships."

JR was not happy about the passive attack on sales. But as usual, he didn't respond.

Kathryn did. "Have you guys looked at your competitors' web sites?" A few of them nodded, not knowing what she was getting at. "Do you know the track records of the people who are running those companies?" Blank looks on their faces. "Exactly. They don't have heavy hitters on their teams. Why do you think that they are making more progress than you are?"

Jeff gave a half-hearted explanation. "Well, Wired Vineyard lined up a partnership with Hewlett-Packard right out of the gate. And Telecart is getting most of its revenue from professional services at this point."

Kathryn seemed unconvinced. "And? What's stopping you from forming a partnership or adjusting your business plan like they did?"

Jan raised her hand to speak but didn't wait for Kathryn to acknowledge her. "Don't take this wrong, Kathryn. But could you start saying *us* and *we* instead of *you?* You're the CEO, and you're part of our team now."

The room stopped, waiting to see how Kathryn would handle the pointed comment. She looked down into her lap, as if she were trying to decide how to respond, and then looked back up. "You're right, Jan. I'm not a consultant here. Thanks for calling me on it. I guess I just don't feel like I'm part of the group yet."

"Join the club."

Jan's response caught everyone off guard.

"What do you mean by that?" asked Nick.

"Well, I don't know about you guys, but I don't feel connected to what's going on outside of finance. Sometimes I feel like a consultant myself. At other companies where I've worked I've always been more involved in sales and operations, and right now, I feel isolated in my own area."

Carlos agreed with her. "Yeah, it does seem like we don't really have the same goals in mind when we're at staff meetings. It almost feels like we're all lobbying for more resources for our departments, or trying to avoid getting involved in anything outside our own areas."

It was hard for anyone to argue with Carlos's logic. He continued, "And you guys think I'm such a prince for volunteering, but that's how everyone works at most of the companies I've worked for."

Kathryn was relieved to see that a few of the people on the team were breaking through, which is why she was so blindsided by the reaction to her next remark. "The politics around here are astounding, and they're a result of everyone being far too ambiguous about what we're all trying to accomplish, and that makes it easy to focus on individual success."

Nick was frowning now. "Wait a second. I agree that

we're not the most healthy group of executives in the Valley, but don't you think you're going a little too far when you say we're political?"

"No. I think that this is one of the most political groups I've ever seen." As the words came out of her mouth, Kathryn realized that she probably could have been a little more delicate. Right away she could sense the people in the room banding together to challenge her harsh critique.

Even Jeff took issue. "I don't know, Kathryn. This might be a function of your not having worked in high tech. I've worked at some pretty political companies in the past, and I don't know if we're all that bad."

Kathryn wanted to respond, but decided to let the others empty their chambers first.

Nick fired away. "I think we're about average, based on what I've heard from other executives. Keep in mind, this is a tough market."

Smelling blood in the water now, Mikey dove in. "I agree. I mean, you've joined the company at a weird time, and to make that statement after just a few weeks is pretty careless." Although her colleagues didn't agree with the harshness of that remark, Mikey knew that they weren't going to challenge her on this one and risk wasting an opportunity to regain a little of the upper hand with their new boss.

Kathryn waited until no more comments came, and then responded. "First of all, I am sorry if my comment sounded flip. You're right in that I haven't worked in high tech, and so my reference point could be a little off." She let the partial apology sink in before continuing and made sure not to begin her next sentence with the word *but*. "And I certainly don't want to come across as condescending to you, because that doesn't help us get where we need to go."

Kathryn sensed that a few of the team members—Jan, Carlos, and Jeff—received her statement in the sincere vein in which it was intended.

She continued. "At the same time, I don't want to downplay the very dangerous situation that we're all in. We have big problems, and I've observed enough of this group to know that politics are alive and well here." As graciously as she acknowledged the concerns of her people, Kathryn was certainly not backing down. "And frankly, I would rather overstate the problem than understate it. But only for the good of the team, not for my own satisfaction. I can assure you of that."

Because of her consistent behavior over the past day and a half, and the confidence with which Kathryn made her remark, most of her staff seemed convinced that she was sincere.

Nick frowned, but Kathryn couldn't tell if he was angry or confused. It was confusion. "Maybe you should tell us exactly what you mean by politics."

Kathryn thought for just a moment and then answered as though she were reciting from a book she had memorized.

"Politics is when people choose their words and actions based on how they want others to react rather than based on what they really think."

The room was silent.

Martin, as serious as ever, cut through the tension. "Okay, we're definitely political." Though he had not intended to be funny, Carlos and Jan laughed out loud. Jeff just smiled and nodded his head.

As compelling as the points she was making were, Kathryn could see that members of the group were still trying to decide whether to embrace her ideas, or attack them. It became immediately clear that the next move would be an attack.

ATTACK

To Kathryn's surprise, it was JR who challenged her, and he wasn't particularly nice. "I'm sorry, but you're not going to make us wait for three weeks to find out what the other dysfunctions are, are you? Can you just tell us what they are so we can figure out what's not working and get on with it?"

Taken at face value, the comment would have been somewhat innocuous. Maybe even a compliment if it were offered in the spirit of true curiosity. But in that moment, with the tone in which it was asked, and given the usually mellow nature of the person who posed the question, it was the harshest comment thus far of the off-site.

Had Kathryn been a less secure executive, she would have been rocked by the remark. And for a moment, she almost let herself get disappointed that the goodwill she thought she was generating had dissipated so quickly. But then she realized that this was precisely what she needed in order to provoke real change in the group: honest resistance.

As much as she wanted to stick to her plan and gradually unveil her simple model, Kathryn decided to take JR's advice. "No problem. Let's go through the other three dysfunctions right now."

EXHIBITION

Kathryn went to the white board, but before she filled in the second box from the bottom, she asked the group a question. "Why do you think that trust is important? What's the practical downside for a group that doesn't trust one another?"

After a few seconds of silence, Jan tried to help Kathryn out. "Morale problems. Inefficiency."

"That's a little too general. I'm looking for one very specific reason why trust is necessary."

No one seemed ready to offer an answer, so Kathryn quickly provided it for them. Just above *absence of trust* she wrote *fear of conflict*.

"If we don't trust one another, then we aren't going to engage in open, constructive, ideological conflict. And we'll just continue to preserve a sense of artificial harmony."

Nick challenged. "But we seem to have plenty of conflict. And not a lot of harmony, I might add."

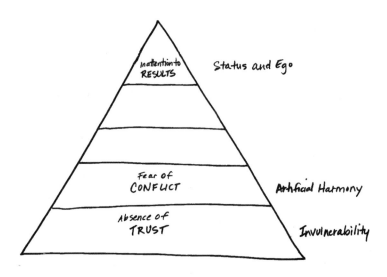

Kathryn shook her head. "No. You have tension. But there is almost no constructive conflict. Passive, sarcastic comments are not the kind of conflict I'm talking about."

Carlos weighed in. "But why is harmony a problem?"

"It's the lack of conflict that's a problem. Harmony itself is good, I suppose, if it comes as a result of working through issues constantly and cycling through conflict. But if it comes only as a result of people holding back their opinions and honest concerns, then it's a bad thing. I'd trade that false kind of harmony any day for a team's willingness to argue effectively about an issue and then walk away with no collateral damage."

Carlos accepted the explanation.

Kathryn pressed her luck. "After watching a few of your

staff meetings, I can say with a degree of confidence that you don't argue very well. Your frustration sometimes surfaces in the form of subtle comments, but more often than not, it is bottled up and carried around. Am I right?"

Instead of answering her semi-rhetorical question and giving Kathryn a modicum of satisfaction, Martin prodded her. "So let's say we start arguing more. I don't see how that is going to make us more effective. If anything, it's going to take up a lot more time."

Mikey and JR were nodding now. Kathryn was ready to take them on, but Jan and Carlos stepped in for her.

First Jan. "Don't you think we're wasting time as it is by not hashing things out? How long have we been talking about outsourcing IT? I think it comes up at every meeting, and half of us are for it, half are against it, and so it just sits there because no one wants to piss anyone off."

Carlos added with a sense of conviction that he rarely showed, "And ironically, that is exactly what pisses us off!"

Martin was growing more and more convinced and wanted to learn about the rest of the model. "Okay, what's the next one?" That was as close to an acknowledgment of being right as Kathryn was going to get from Martin.

Kathryn went back to the white board. "The next dysfunction of a team is the *lack of commitment* and the failure to buy in to decisions." She wrote the dysfunction above the previous one. "And the evidence of this one is *ambiguity,*" which she wrote next to it.

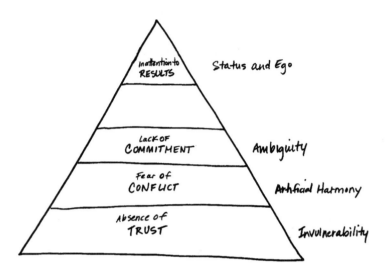

Nick was reengaging now. "Commitment? Sounds like something my wife complained about before we got married." The group chuckled at his mediocre joke.

Kathryn was ready for the reaction. "I'm talking about committing to a plan or a decision, and getting everyone to clearly buy in to it. That's why conflict is so important."

As smart as he was, Martin was not afraid to admit his confusion. "I don't get it."

Kathryn explained, "It's as simple as this. When people don't unload their opinions and feel like they've been listened to, they won't really get on board."

"They do if you make them," countered Nick. "I'm guessing your husband doesn't let his players vote on whether they want to run wind-sprints."

Kathryn welcomed this kind of challenge. "No, he doesn't. But he'd let them make a case why they think they shouldn't. And if he disagreed with them, which in that situation I'm sure he would, he'd tell them why and then send them off running."

"So this isn't a consensus thing." Jan's statement was really a question.

"Heavens no," insisted Kathryn, sounding like a school teacher again. "Consensus is horrible. I mean, if everyone really agrees on something and consensus comes about quickly and naturally, well that's terrific. But that isn't how it usually works, and so consensus becomes an attempt to please everyone."

"Which usually turns into displeasing everyone equally." Jeff made his remark with a look of pain on his face, as though he were reliving a bad memory.

"Exactly. The point here is that most reasonable people don't have to get their way in a discussion. They just need to be heard, and to know that their input was considered and responded to."

"So where does the lack of commitment come into play?" Nick wanted to know.

"Well, some teams get paralyzed by their need for complete agreement, and their inability to move beyond debate."

JR spoke up. "Disagree and commit."

"Excuse me?" Kathryn wanted him to explain.

"Yeah, in my last company we called it 'disagree and commit.' You can argue about something and disagree, but still commit to it as though everyone originally bought into the decision completely."

That lit a bulb in Jeff. "Okay, I see where conflict fits in. Even if people are generally willing to commit, they aren't going to do so because . . ."

Carlos interrupted. " . . . because they need to weigh in before they can really buy in."

The room seemed to understand that.

"What's the last dysfunction?" Everyone was surprised that it was Mikey who asked, and she actually seemed interested in the answer.

Kathryn went to the board to fill in the last empty box. Before she could, Martin had opened his laptop and started typing. Everyone froze. Kathryn stopped and looked at her chief technologist, who seemed clueless about the new sense of tension in the room.

And then suddenly it dawned on him. "Oh no, I'm actually, uh, I really am taking notes about this. Look." He was attempting to show everyone the document that he was creating on his screen.

Everyone was amused at Martin's anxiety about explaining his behavior and not wanting to violate the team rules. Kathryn laughed, pleased that her engineer was suddenly enthusiastic about what was going on. "That's okay. We believe you. I'll let it slide this time."

Kathryn looked at her watch and realized that the group hadn't taken a break for several hours. "It's late. Let's go ahead and break for a half-hour. We'll finish this later."

Though they would deny it if asked, Kathryn was certain that she saw disappointment on the faces of everyone in the room. JR was big enough to admit it. "Let's go ahead and do the last one." And then he added humorously, "I don't think any of us are going to be able to relax if we don't know what it is."

As sarcastic as the comment could have sounded, buried just below the humor was a subtle but unmistakable sense of acknowledgment. Whether he was acknowledging the rudeness of his prior statement or the validity of what Kathryn was explaining didn't seem as important as the tone of the comment itself.

Kathryn was glad to oblige. She went to the board for the last time and wrote *avoidance of accountability*.

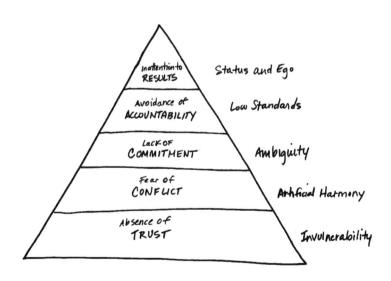

She explained. "Once we achieve clarity and buy-in, it is then that we have to hold each other accountable for what we sign up to do, for high standards of performance and behavior. And as simple as that sounds, most executives hate to do it, especially when it comes to a peer's behavior, because they want to avoid interpersonal discomfort."

"What exactly do you mean by that?" Jeff asked.

"I'm talking about that moment when you know you have to call one of your peers on something that matters, and you decide to let it go because you just don't want to experience that feeling when . . ." She paused, and Martin finished the sentence for her: " . . . when you have to tell someone to shut down their e-mail during meetings."

"Exactly," Kathryn confirmed appreciatively.

Carlos added, "I hate this one. I just don't want to have to tell someone that their standards are too low. I'd rather just tolerate it and avoid the . . ." He tried to think of the right way to describe it.

Jan did it for him: " . . . the interpersonal discomfort."

Carlos nodded. "Yeah, I guess that's really what it is." He thought about it for a moment, then continued. "But it's weird. I don't have as much of a problem telling my direct reports what I think. I seem to hold them accountable most of the time, even when it's a sticky issue."

Kathryn was thrilled by the remark. "Right. As hard as it is sometimes to enter the danger with your direct reports and confront them with something sticky, it's even harder with your peers."

"Why's that?" asked Jeff.

Before Kathryn could answer, Nick explained. "Because we're supposed to be equals. And who am I to tell Martin how to do his job, or Mikey, or Jan? It feels like I'm sticking my nose into their business when I do."

Kathryn explained further. "The peer-to-peer thing is certainly one of the issues that makes team accountability hard. But there's something else."

No one seemed to have a clue, and Kathryn was ready to answer her own question. Just then Mikey's face lit up like she had just solved a puzzle. "No buy-in."

"What?" asked Nick.

"No buy-in. People aren't going to hold each other accountable if they haven't clearly bought in to the same plan. Otherwise, it seems pointless because they're just going to say, 'I never agreed to that anyway.'"

Kathryn was shocked at her unlikely star pupil. And if that wasn't enough, Mikey went on to say, "This actually makes sense."

Everyone looked at one another as if to say, *Did you hear what I heard?*

On that note, Kathryn excused the team for their last break of the day.

FILM NOIR

No matter how many times Kathryn had built or refurbished teams, she never got used to watching the inevitable ebbs and flows. *Why can't we just make progress in one fell swoop?* she asked herself.

In theory, with Mikey and Martin now seemingly on board, it should have been relatively easy to make the team work. But Kathryn knew that reality did not usually match theory; she still had a long way to go. Two years of behavioral reinforcement around politics is a tough thing to break, and one lecture, no matter how compelling, is not going to do it. The painful, heavy lifting was still to come.

With just a few hours until the end of the first off-site, Kathryn was tempted to end the session early and send everyone back to work on a relative high. But that would have been a waste of two critical hours, she thought. She needed to make as much progress as possible, and soon, to ensure that the board wouldn't be tempted to cut her effort short.

When the group had returned from their break, Kathryn decided to introduce a relatively entertaining discussion topic relating to conflict, one that would hold their interest late in the day.

"Let's talk more about conflict."

She felt the room sink just a little at the prospect of taking on such a touchy subject. But Kathryn was actually looking forward to this part.

"Someone tell me what the single most important arena or setting for conflict is."

After a pause, Nick took a stab. "Meetings?"

"Yes. Meetings. If we cannot learn to engage in productive, ideological conflict during meetings, we are through."

Jan smiled.

"And I'm not joking when I say that. Our ability to engage in passionate, unfiltered debate about what we need to do to succeed will determine our future as much as any products we develop or partnerships we sign."

It was late afternoon now, and Kathryn sensed that her team was drifting into postlunch food coma. Her words didn't seem to be getting through to them, and she would have to make this interesting if she had any chance of making it stick.

"How many of you would rather go to a meeting than a movie?"

No hands went up.

"Why not?"

After a pause, Jeff realized that her question was not a rhetorical one. "Because movies are more interesting. Even the bad ones."

His peers chuckled.

Kathryn smiled. "Right. But if you really think about it, meetings should be at least as interesting as movies. My son, Will, went to film school, and I learned from him that meetings and movies have a lot in common."

The group seemed more doubtful than intrigued, but at least Kathryn had their interest for the moment. "Think about it this way. A movie, on average, runs anywhere from ninety minutes to two hours in length. Staff meetings are about the same."

Heads nodded, politely.

"And yet meetings are interactive, whereas movies are not. We can't yell at the actor on the screen, 'Don't go into the house you idiot!'"

Most of the group laughed. *Are they actually starting to like me?* Kathryn wondered in a brief and uncharacteristic moment of insecurity.

She went on. "And more importantly, movies have no real impact on our lives. They don't require us to act a certain way based on the outcome of the story. And yet meetings are both interactive and relevant. We get to have our say, and the outcome of any given discussion often has a very real impact on our lives. So why do we dread meetings?"

No one answered, so Kathryn prodded them. "Come on, why do we hate them?"

"They're boring." Mikey seemed to enjoy her answer more than she should have.

"Right. They're boring. And to understand why, all we need to do is compare them to films."

Now the group was starting to get interested again. Kathryn continued. "Whether it is an action movie, a drama, a comedy, or an artsy French film, every movie worth watching must have one key ingredient. What is that ingredient?"

Martin answered dryly. "Well, since we're talking about conflict, I'm guessing that's it."

"Yes, I suppose that I telegraphed that one, didn't I? Every great movie has conflict. Without it, we just don't care what happens to the characters."

Kathryn paused for effect before delivering her next line. "Let me assure you that from now on, every staff meeting we have will be loaded with conflict. And they won't be boring. And if there is nothing worth debating, then we won't have a meeting."

The team seemed to like that statement, and Kathryn wanted to deliver on her promise immediately. "And so we're going to start right now." She checked her watch. "We have almost two hours until we break today, and so I thought I would have our first substantive decision-making meeting as a group."

Nick objected, with a serious look on his face. "Kathryn, I'm not sure I can do this." Caught off guard, everyone waited for an explanation. "I never received an agenda."

Everyone, including Jeff, laughed at the good-natured teasing of their former CEO.

APPLICATION

athryn wasted no time. "Okay, here's the deal. Before we leave this meeting, we are going to establish something I call our overarching goal for the rest of the year. There is no reason that we can't do this now, right here, today. Someone take a stab."

"What do you mean exactly?" Jan asked. "Like a theme?"

"Yeah. The question we need to answer is this: If we do anything between now and the end of the year, what should that be?"

Nick and JR responded in unison. "Market share."

Heads around the table nodded, except Martin's and Jan's. Kathryn called them out.

"You two don't seem convinced. What are you thinking?"

Martin explained, "I think it's product improvement."

Jan added, "And I'm not so sure that cost containment isn't our top priority."

Kathryn resisted the temptation to address their suggestions herself. "Someone take them on."

JR obliged. "Okay, I think that our technology is as good as, or better than, both of our top competitors'. And yet, they are getting more traction than we are. If we fall too far behind in terms of market capture, it won't matter what our products can do."

Martin barely frowned. "If that's the case, then imagine what things would look like if we fell behind in products."

Ever the peacemaker, Carlos asked, "Can't we have more than one overarching goal?"

Kathryn shook her head. "If everything is important, then nothing is." She resisted any further explanation, wanting the group to work through it.

Jan persisted. "Can someone tell me why cost containment isn't the goal?"

Mikey responded quickly. "Because if we don't find a way to make money, avoiding spending it does us no good." As annoying as Mikey's tone was, the truth of the statement could not be denied. Even Jan nodded in concession.

Kathryn made a quick comment. "This is the most productive conversation I've heard since I've been here. Keep going."

That was enough to give Jeff the courage he needed to make his point. He winced, as though he didn't want to prolong the conversation. "I don't know. I'm not sure that market share is the right measure at this point. We don't really know what the size of the market is and where it's headed." He paused while he decided what to say next. "I think we just need more good customers. Whether we have twenty more or twenty less than our competition doesn't seem to matter as much."

Mikey jumped in. "That's the same as market share."

"I don't think so," Jeff offered nondefensively.

Mikey rolled her eyes.

Nick wanted to avoid a repeat of the previous day's encounter with Mikey. "Listen, whether we call it market share or customers doesn't really matter. We just need to sell."

Now Kathryn spoke. "I think it matters. What do you think, JR?"

"I think Jeff is right. If we get enough solid customers, the kind who will be active references for us, then we're doing fine. Frankly, I don't care at this point what our competition is doing. That seems like a distraction more than anything else—at least until we get rolling and the market takes shape."

Martin seemed annoyed now. "Listen, this is the same kind of conversation we have at every meeting. If it's not market share versus revenue, it's customer retention versus satisfaction. It all seems academic to me."

Kathryn forced herself to be silent for a few moments as the room digested Martin's comment. Then she asked, "How do those conversations usually end?"

Martin shrugged. "We run out of time, I guess."

"Okay. Let's bring this conversation to a close in the next five minutes. Does anyone here believe that the key to the next nine months has something to do with market share, customers, revenue, et cetera? If someone thinks we're in the wrong ballpark completely, speak up now, and loudly."

People looked at one another and shrugged as if to say, *I can't think of anything better.*

"Good. Then let's come to closure on exactly what we're talking about. I'd like to hear someone make a passionate plea for the answer being revenue. JR, how about you?"

"Well, one might argue that revenue is the right answer, because we need cash. But frankly, I think that is far less important at this point than proving to the world that there are customers out there who are interested in our products. Revenue is not as important as closing deals and getting new customers." He had just talked himself out of the revenue answer. "Does that make sense?"

"It makes perfect sense to me." Kathryn pushed on for clarity. "So I'm not hearing anyone saying that revenue is our most important goal."

Jan squinted and spoke up. "Are you saying that we don't need to have a revenue goal?"

"No. We will definitely have a revenue goal. It's just that revenue is not the ultimate measure of our success right now. We've narrowed it down to market share and new customers. Someone tell me why market share is the right answer. Mikey?"

"Market share is how analysts and the press define success. It's as simple as that."

Martin countered. "No, Mikey. Whenever I'm interviewed as a founder of the company, people ask me about key customers. They want marquee company names and people who are willing to vouch for us."

Mikey shrugged.

Kathryn challenged her. "Are you shrugging because you don't agree and you're giving up, or because you feel like he made a more compelling point than you can counter?"

Mikey thought about it. "The second one."

"Okay. We're down to new customer acquisition. Someone tell me why this should be our collective, overarching goal."

This time Kathryn didn't need to call anyone out. Carlos volunteered.

"Because that will give the press something to write about. It will give our employees confidence. It will provide more product feedback for Martin and his engineers. And it will give us references to go out and get more customers next year."

JR chimed in. "Not to mention follow-on sales."

"Ladies and gentlemen," Kathryn announced, "unless I hear something extremely compelling in the next five seconds that makes me think otherwise, I believe we have a primary goal."

Members of the staff looked at each other as if to say, *Are we really agreeing on something?*

But Kathryn wasn't through yet. She wanted specifics. "How many new customers do we need to get?"

The group seemed to be invigorated by the tangible nature of the discussion. For the next thirty minutes, they debated the number of new customers they could and should acquire.

Jan lobbied for the most, followed by Nick and Mikey. JR was frustrated and argued hard for the fewest, wanting to keep his quota low so as not to discourage his salespeople. Jeff, Carlos, and Martin were somewhere in between.

As the debate seemed to be running out of steam, Kathryn jumped in. "Okay, unless someone is holding something back, I think I've heard all the opinions in the room. And we are probably not going to agree completely, which is fine, because there is no science here. I'm going to set the number based on your input, and we are going to stick with that number."

She paused for a moment, then continued. "Jan, we aren't going to do thirty deals this year, even though I know how much you'd love that revenue on the books. And JR, I can appreciate your desire to keep your folks motivated, but ten is not enough. Our competitors are doing more than double that, and the analysts will throw up all over us if we come in at ten."

JR seemed to offer no resistance to Kathryn's logic.

She continued. "I think that if we can close eighteen new customers, with at least ten being willing to be active references, we will be doing well."

She paused to allow any last comments. When none came, she declared, "All right then. We will have eighteen new customers by December 31."

No one could deny that in twenty minutes the team had made more progress than they normally did during a month of meetings. Over the next hour they drilled down on the issue of new customers, discussing what each person, from marketing to finance to engineering, would need to do to make eighteen deals possible.

With fifteen minutes to spare before the off-site was to officially end, Kathryn decided to bring things to a close. "Okay, let's call it a day. We'll be having a staff meeting next week when we can dig deeper into some of these and other critical issues."

The group seemed relieved to be finished. Kathryn asked one final question. "Are there any comments, questions, or concerns people want to raise before we leave?"

No one wanted to bring up a topic that would delay their departures, but Nick decided to make one comment. "I have to say that I think we made more progress during these past two days than I thought we would."

Jan and Carlos nodded in agreement. Mikey, to everyone's surprise, didn't roll her eyes.

Kathryn wasn't sure whether Nick was trying to make points with her, or whether he really appreciated what had happened. She decided to give him the benefit of the doubt and take the muted compliment to heart.

And then JR spoke. "I agree with Nick. We accomplished a lot here, and getting clarity around our major goal is really going to help."

Kathryn sensed that there was a qualifier coming. And she was right.

JR continued. "I'm just wondering if we need to continue having these off-sites now. I mean, we've come a long way, and we're going to have to do a lot of work over the next few months to close deals. Maybe we can just see how things go . . ."

He didn't really finish the remark, but let it hang there. Martin, Mikey, and Nick were cautiously nodding their heads in agreement.

Whatever sense of accomplishment that Kathryn had felt just a few minutes earlier had diminished significantly. As much as she wanted to put a quick and violent end to JR's suggestion, Kathryn waited to see if anyone would do it for her. Just when she thought no one would help her, Jeff spoke up and demonstrated that he had indeed taken many of Kathryn's ideas to heart.

"I'd have to say that canceling our next session in two weeks would be a bad idea. I just think that when we go back to work, it's going to be easy to slip back into the same stuff we've been struggling with for the past couple years. And as painful as it's been for me to sit here for the past few days and realize how unsuccessful I've been in making us work like a team, we have a long way to go yet."

Jan and Carlos nodded their agreement.

Kathryn used the opportunity to prepare her team for what was to come. She addressed her initial comment to

JR and Nick. "I appreciate your desire to spend as much of your time as possible closing deals." She was being slightly disingenuous but wanted to avoid slamming them too hard, too early. "However, I want to remind you about what I said at the beginning of this session yesterday. We have more money, better technology, and more talented and experienced executives than our competitors, and yet we are behind. What we lack is teamwork, and I can promise you all that I have no greater priority as CEO than making you, I mean, us, more effective as a group."

Mikey, Martin, and Nick seemed to be relenting now, but Kathryn continued. "And what I'm about to say is more important than any other comment I've made since we arrived yesterday." She paused for effect. "During the next two weeks I am going to be pretty intolerant of behavior that demonstrates an absence of trust, or a focus on individual ego. I will be encouraging conflict, driving for clear commitments, and expecting all of you to hold each other accountable. I will be calling out bad behavior when I see it, and I'd like to see you doing the same. We don't have time to waste."

The room was silent.

"Okay, we'll be back here again in two weeks. Drive carefully everyone, and I'll see you in the office tomorrow."

As everyone packed up and headed for the door, Kathryn wanted to feel good about what she had accomplished. However, she forced herself to face the likely prospect that things would have to get worse, maybe even much worse, before they would get better.

Even most of the staff members seemed to be sobered by the likely prospect of ongoing pain. And none of them would have been surprised to know that one of their colleagues wouldn't be around by the time the next off-site began. They would have been shocked, however, to know that the colleague would not be Mikey.

PART THREE

Heavy Lifting

ON-SITE

ack in the office, even Kathryn was surprised by the rapid deterioration of any progress that had been made during the off-site.

The few glimmers of hope that did surface—like Carlos and Martin having a joint customer satisfaction meeting with their staffs—were enough to get employees whispering about what was going on. But in Kathryn's mind, there was no denying that the team was still guarded with one another, and with her.

Based on the hallway demeanor she observed, Kathryn felt as though the team had completely forgotten about their two days in Napa. There was little interaction, and almost no signs of willingness to engage with one another. The team seemed as though they were embarrassed by having exposed themselves and were pretending that it had never happened at all.

But Kathryn had been through this many times before. And as disappointed as she was that the group had not completely internalized the concepts from the off-site, she knew that this was a typical first response. She also knew that the only way to defuse it would be to dive right back in and get the group's blood flowing again. She had no idea that she was about to hit an artery.

It happened just a few days after the off-site had ended, on the same day that Kathryn's first official staff meeting would later take place.

Nick had called a special meeting to discuss a possible acquisition. He invited anyone on the team who was interested to attend but made it clear that he needed Kathryn, Martin, JR, and Jeff to be there. Jan and Carlos also showed up.

Before starting the meeting, Nick asked, "Where's JR?"

"He's not in the office this morning." Kathryn said. "Let's get started."

Nick shrugged and then began passing around a stack of glossy brochures to his colleagues. "The company is called Green Banana." The group laughed.

"I know. Where do they get these names? Anyway, they're a company in Boston that is either complementary to us or a potential competitor. It's tough to say. In any case, I think we should consider acquiring them. They are hurting for cash, and we've got more than we need at this point."

Jeff, feeling more like a board member than anything else, asked the first question. "What would we get?"

Nick, who had already decided that the deal made sense, answered quickly. "Customers. Employees. Technology."

"How many customers?" Kathryn wanted to know.

Martin asked another question before Nick could answer the first one. "And is their technology good? I've never heard of them."

Nick again had quick answers. "They're about half our size in terms of customers." He read his notes. "About twenty, I think. And their technology is apparently good enough for those customers."

Martin looked skeptical.

Kathryn frowned. "How many employees? And are they all in Boston?"

"Yes, they have somewhere around seventy-five people, and all but seven of them are in Beantown."

During the Napa off-site meeting, Kathryn had been careful to hold back her opinions in order to develop the skills of her team. But in the heat of real-world decision making, restraint was not her best quality. "Hold on. This doesn't sound right to me, Nick. We would be increasing the size of the firm by 50 percent and adding a whole new set of products. I think we've got plenty of challenges to deal with as it is."

As prepared as Nick was for dissent, he couldn't mask his impatience. "If we don't make bold moves like this, we're going to miss opportunities to distance ourselves from our competitors. We have to be visionaries here."

Now Martin rolled his eyes.

Kathryn pushed on Nick. "First, I need to say that Mikey should have been at this meeting. I'd like to know what she thinks in terms of market positioning and strategy. And I . . ."

Nick interrupted. "Mikey isn't going to add any value to this conversation. This has nothing to do with public relations or advertising. This is strategy."

Kathryn wanted to jump down Nick's throat for being so harsh to someone who wasn't in the room, and everyone could see that. But she decided it could wait for a few minutes. "I wasn't quite finished. I also believe that the issues we currently have around politics would only be exacerbated by an acquisition."

Nick took a deep breath, the kind that says, *I can't believe I have to deal with people like this.* Before he could say something he would regret, Jan jumped in.

"And I understand that our cash position is better than any of our competitors, and better than 90 percent of the technology companies in the Valley. But just because we have it doesn't mean that we should spend it. Not unless it's a clear winner."

Now Nick was about to regret his words. "With all due respect, Kathryn, you might be a fine executive when it comes to leading meetings and improving teamwork. But you don't know squat about our business. I think you should defer to Jeff and me when it comes to things like this."

The room froze. Kathryn was sure that someone would pounce on Nick for his mini-tirade. She was wrong. In fact,

Martin had the audacity to look at his watch and say, "Hey, I'm sorry, but I've got another meeting. Let me know if you need my input." And he left.

Kathryn was perfectly prepared to call any of her reports on destructive behaviors that might hurt the team, but she didn't think the first opportunity would center around her. That made it more difficult, but necessary nonetheless. The question was whether she should do it privately, or in front of the rest of the group.

"Nick, would you rather that we have this conversation right here, or one-on-one?"

He stopped to consider her question carefully, fully aware of what was about to ensue. "I guess I could be macho and say, 'If you have something to say, go ahead.' But I think we should have this one alone." He actually smiled, but only for a split second.

Kathryn asked the rest of the group if they would leave Nick and her alone. "I'll see you this afternoon at the staff meeting." They gladly left.

As soon as they were gone, Kathryn spoke, but in a confident and relaxed way, far more in control than Nick had expected.

"Okay, first of all, don't ever slam one of your teammates when that person isn't in the room. I don't care what you think of Mikey. She is part of this team, and you have to take your issues to her directly, or to me. You're going to have to make that right."

Nick, all six feet three inches of him, looked like a seventh grader in the principal's office. But just for a moment. Then he regained his frustration and shot back at Kathryn. "Look, I've got nothing to do around here. We were supposed to be growing much faster by now and getting involved in a lot more M&A activity. I can't just sit around and watch this place . . ."

Kathryn interrupted. "So this is about you?"

Nick didn't seem to hear her question. "What?"

"This acquisition. It's about you wanting to have something to do?"

Nick tried to backtrack. "No, I think it's a good idea. It could be strategic for us."

Kathryn just sat and listened, and like a criminal being interrogated, Nick started to spill his guts. "But yes, I am completely underutilized here. I moved my family halfway across this damn country with the expectation that I might someday be able to run this place, and now I am bored, helpless, and watching my peers screw this thing up." Nick was looking down now, shaking his head out of both guilt and disbelief at his situation.

Kathryn calmly addressed his comment. "Do you think you're contributing to screwing this thing up?"

He looked up. "No. I mean, I'm supposed to be in charge of infrastructure growth, mergers and acquisitions. We're not doing any of that because the board says . . ."

"I'm talking about the bigger picture, Nick. Are you

making this team better, or are you contributing to the dys-function?"

"What do you think?"

"I don't think you're making it better." She paused. "You clearly have a lot to offer, whether or not you ever run this place."

Nick tried to explain. "I wasn't trying to say that I want your job. I was just venting and . . ."

Kathryn held up her hand. "Don't worry about it. You're allowed to vent from time to time. But I have to tell you that I don't see you stepping up and helping people. If anything, you're tearing them down."

Nick wasn't ready to buy what Kathryn was saying. He argued, "So what do you think I should do?"

"Why don't you try telling the rest of the group where you're coming from. Tell them what you just told me, about feeling underutilized and moving your family across . . ."

"That doesn't have anything to do with whether we acquire Green Banana or not."

They both smiled for just a moment at the ridiculous name.

Nick continued. "I mean, if they don't understand why we need to be doing things like this, then maybe . . ." He hesitated.

Kathryn finished his thought. "Maybe what? Maybe you should quit?"

Nick was hot now. "Is that what you want? If that's what you want, then maybe I will."

Kathryn just sat there, letting the situation sink in for Nick. Then she said, "It's not about what I want. It's about you. You have to decide what is more important: helping the team win or advancing your career."

Even Kathryn thought she sounded a little harsh, but she knew what she was doing.

"I don't see why those have to be mutually exclusive," Nick argued.

"They're not. It's just that one has to be more important than the other."

Nick looked at the wall, shaking his head, trying to decide whether he should be mad at Kathryn or thank her for forcing his hand. "Whatever." He stood and left the room.

FIREWORKS

By two o'clock, everyone was seated around the table in the main conference room waiting for the staff meeting to begin—everyone, that is, except Nick and JR. Kathryn checked her watch and decided to get started. "Okay, today we'll do a quick review of what everyone is working on, and then spend most of our time laying the groundwork for the eighteen deals we need to close."

Jeff was about to ask Kathryn where Nick and JR were when Nick walked in the room.

"Sorry I'm late." There were two empty seats at the table—one next to Kathryn and the other at the opposite end. He chose the one away from the CEO.

Given what had happened earlier in the day, Kathryn was not about to scold Nick for being late. The rest of the team seemed to understand her restraint. Instead, she launched into the meeting. "Before we get started, I need to . . ."

Then Nick interrupted. "I've got something to say."

Everyone knew that Nick could be rude. But the way he had just interrupted Kathryn—and after arriving late to her first official staff meeting—seemed particularly audacious to the staff. Oddly enough, Kathryn didn't seem flustered at all.

Nick began, "Listen, I need to get some things off my chest here."

No one moved. Inside, they were boiling with anticipation.

"First, about the meeting this morning. I was out of line. I should have made sure that Mikey was there, and that comment I made about her was not fair."

Mikey was stunned, and then angry, but said nothing.

Nick addressed her. "Don't get all pushed out of shape, Mikey. I'll tell you about it later. It's not that big of a deal."

Strangely, Mikey actually seemed reassured by Nick's candor and confidence.

He continued. "Second, as much as I believe that Green Banana might be something we want to consider, my insistence on doing the deal is more about giving me something to work on. See, I'm beginning to feel that I made a bad career move by coming here, and I just want something that I can hang my hat on. I don't know how I'm going to explain what I've been doing for the past eighteen months on my resumé."

Jan looked at Kathryn, the only person in the room who didn't seem shocked.

Nick continued. "But I think it's time I faced the reality of the situation and made a decision." He paused before going on. "I need to make a change. I need to find a way to contribute to this team, and this company. And I need you guys to help me. Otherwise, I should leave. But I'm not ready to do that just yet."

Kathryn would have liked to claim that she knew that Nick would come around, but she would later admit to her husband that she honestly believed he would quit. Being wrong notwithstanding, she was suddenly thrilled that he was staying. And she couldn't quite explain why.

The room was silent, not knowing how to respond to the statement that was out of character for both Nick and the team. Kathryn wanted to congratulate Nick for being so open but decided to let the moment speak for itself. When it became clear that the team had fully digested the magnitude of the situation and had nothing more to add, Kathryn went ahead and broke the silence. "I need to make an announcement."

Martin was sure he was about to witness a group hug, or some sort of touchy-feely, conciliatory comment from Kathryn. Until she completed her thought. "JR quit last night."

If the room was quiet when Nick finished speaking, it was dead now. But only for a few long seconds.

"What?" It was Martin who reacted first. "Why?"

"It's not completely clear," explained Kathryn. "At least

not based on what he told me. Evidently, he's gone back to AddSoft to be a regional VP again." Kathryn hesitated before her next comment, which she considered withholding, but decided wouldn't be right. "He also told me he just didn't want to waste any more of his time at off-site meetings working out people's personal problems."

Another heavy moment. Kathryn waited.

Mikey spoke first. "Okay, does anyone else here think that this team-building stuff has gone too far? Are we making things better, or worse?"

Even Carlos raised his eyebrows, as though he were entertaining Mikey's comment. The momentum in the room seemed tangible now, and it was moving away from Kathryn.

After the longest three seconds in Kathryn's brief career at DecisionTech, Martin weighed in. "Well, I don't think it's news to anyone here that I hate doing this team stuff. I mean, it's like fingernails on a bloody chalkboard to me."

Kathryn didn't need this.

Then Martin finished. "But that's the biggest crock of shit I've ever heard. I think JR was just afraid that he didn't know how to sell this stuff."

Jeff agreed. "He did admit to me a few months ago, over beers in an airport, mind you, that he has never had to sell into a market that didn't already exist. And that he preferred having a brand name behind him. He also said that he had never failed in his life, and that he wasn't about to do so here."

Jan added, "And he hated when we asked him about sales. He felt like we were pounding on him."

Mikey chimed in. "Most of the sales that we have closed were done by Martin and Jeff, anyway. I don't think that guy ever really knew how to . . ."

Kathryn was just about to jump in, when Nick spoke up. "Listen, I know I should be the last person to say this because I was JR's biggest critic behind the scenes, but let's not do this. He's gone, and we need to figure out what we're going to do."

Carlos volunteered. "I'll take over sales until we can find someone else."

Jan felt comfortable enough with Carlos to be direct with him, even in front of the rest of the group. "As much as we appreciate your offer, I think that there are two other people in this room with more time on their hands and more experience with selling." She looked at Jeff who was sitting next to Nick. "One of you two."

Jeff responded immediately. "Don't get me wrong. I'd do whatever you want me to. But I've never run a sales organization, or carried a quota for that matter. I love to sell to investors and even customers, as long as I'm with someone who knows what they're doing."

Mikey offered her opinion. "Nick, you ran field operations at your last company. And you headed a sales team earlier in your career."

Nick nodded.

Martin added, "But I remember when we interviewed

Nick." Martin often referred to people in the third person, as though they weren't sitting in the same room. It wasn't intentionally rude, just less personal. "He said that he wanted to break away from his career label as a field guy. He wanted to take on a more corporate, central leadership role."

Nick nodded again, quietly impressed that Martin had remembered anything about him. "That's right. I felt like I was being pigeon-holed in sales and field ops."

No one spoke for a moment. Nick continued. "But I have to say that I was damn good at sales, and I enjoyed it."

Kathryn resisted the temptation to begin selling Nick. Jeff didn't. "You do have a good relationship with the sales force already. And you have to admit that you've been frustrated by our inability to get into more deals."

Carlos joked. "Come on Nick. If you don't do it, they're going to accept my offer."

Kathryn shrugged at Nick to say, *He's right.*

"In that case it would be negligent of me to say no."

Everyone laughed, when suddenly a fire alarm sounded.

Jan slapped her forehead. "Oh, I forgot. We're having a fire drill today. The Half Moon Bay Fire Department said we have to start doing these twice a year."

Everyone slowly gathered their things.

Martin added a final bit of humor. "Thank God. I could feel a group hug coming on any minute."

LEAKS

A few days later, Kathryn began having problems with her laptop, so she called the IT department to see if anyone there could fix it. The IT department was really just four people, headed by a guy named Brendan, one of Jan's direct reports. Given the size of the group, it wasn't unusual for Brendan to handle some calls himself. Especially if the call came from an executive. Especially the CEO.

Brendan arrived promptly and quickly identified the problem. When he informed Kathryn that he would need to take the computer with him to fix it, she agreed but explained that she would need it back before the end of the week.

"Oh, that's right. You have another off-site coming up."

Kathryn was not surprised that Brendan knew about the off-site. In fact, she was glad that employees knew how her team was spending her time while they were out of the office. But his next comment gave her reason for concern.

"I wish I could be a fly on the wall during those meetings."

Kathryn could not let that comment go without a question. "Oh yeah? Why is that?"

Brendan, whose technical ability was matched only by his lack of social awareness, responded without hesitation. "Well, let's just say that people around here would pay big money to watch Mikey answer for her attitude."

Though Kathryn could not deny feeling slightly glad that others in the organization recognized Mikey's behavioral issues, her primary reaction to Brendan's remark was disappointment. She wondered how many other employees in the company knew details about what was happening at the off-sites.

"Well, I'm not sure that's how I'd characterize what we've been doing."

Kathryn knew that Brendan was not to be blamed for any of this, so she changed the subject. "Anyway, thanks for taking care of my computer."

Brendan left, and Kathryn contemplated how she would handle the situation with Jan, and the rest of the team.

OFF-SITE
NUMBER TWO

The following week, just days after what quickly became known as the Fire Alarm Meeting, the next Napa Valley session began.

Kathryn kicked off the event with her usual speech. "We have more money, better technology, more talented and experienced executives, and yet we're behind our competitors. Let's remember that the reason we're here is to start working more effectively as a team."

Kathryn then raised a difficult topic, but in a tone that was as nonthreatening as she could make it. "I have a quick question for everyone. What, if anything, did you tell your people about the first off-site session we had?"

As hard as she tried, Kathryn could not completely avoid creating an interrogation-like atmosphere in the room. "I'm not here to pound on anyone. I just think we need to get clear on our behaviors as a team."

Jeff went first. "I didn't tell my people anything. Not a single thing."

The room laughed because Jeff no longer had any direct reports.

Mikey went next. "I just said we did a bunch of touchy-feely exercises." She was trying to be funny, but everyone could tell that there was some degree of truth in what she was saying. No one laughed.

Martin suddenly became defensive. "If you have a problem with something we've done, then just tell us. Because I'll admit right now, that I had some pretty frank conversations with my engineers. They want to know whether we're wasting our time or not, and I think they're entitled to an explanation. And if that means violating some degree of confidentiality, then I'm sorry."

The room was a little stunned by the uncharacteristic diatribe, which was both longer and more emotional than what they were used to from Martin.

Kathryn almost laughed. "Whoa. Whoa. I'm not mad at anyone here. And I'm not saying that we shouldn't have talked to our teams about the off-site. In fact, I should have been more explicit last time about our need to do so."

Martin seemed relieved, and a little embarrassed.

Then Jan spoke. "I probably told my team more than anyone else. And I'm guessing that one of them said something to you."

Kathryn felt as though she had been caught by Jan. "Well, in fact, it is one of your people who prompted me to ask this question."

Mikey seemed to enjoy that Jan was being singled out. Kathryn continued, "But this isn't about you or anyone else in particular. I'm just trying to understand how things work in terms of confidentialities and loyalties."

"What do you mean by loyalties?" Nick wanted to know.

"I mean, who do you all consider to be your first team?" Not surprised by the confusion in the room, Kathryn explained. "This is not a lecture about maintaining confidential information. Or at least, that's not the focus of what I'm trying to say. It's beyond that."

Kathryn was getting frustrated by her own inability to articulate the issue. She resorted to bluntness. "What I'm trying to ask you is whether you think this team is as important to you as the teams you lead, your departments."

Suddenly everyone seemed to understand. And they didn't seem comfortable with the true answers in their heads.

Jan asked, "So, you're wondering if we confide in our direct reports about things that we should be keeping between us here?"

Kathryn nodded.

Mikey responded first. "I am much closer to my staff than I am to this group here. I'm sorry, but it's true."

Nick nodded. "I'd probably say that's true for me too, with the exception of the sales group I just took over." He thought about it. "But I'd say that within a few weeks, I'll be closer to them than to this team."

Though Nick's comment was meant as a joke and provoked a shallow laugh among the group, the sad truth of it seemed to deflate the room.

Jan spoke next. "I think all of us would probably say that we consider our teams more important than this one." She hesitated before finishing her thought. "But no one more than me."

That comment grabbed the attention of everyone at the table.

"Do you want to explain that?" Kathryn asked, gently.

"Well, as everyone here knows, I'm pretty tight with my people. Of my eight direct reports, five have worked for me at other companies, and I'm something of a parent to them."

Carlos joked, "She's a den mother."

They laughed.

Jan smiled and nodded her head. "Yeah, I'd have to agree. It's not that I'm overly emotional or anything like that. It's just that they know I'd do almost anything for them."

Kathryn nodded as though she were figuring it all out. "Hmm."

Martin defended Jan. "That's not a bad thing. My engineers know that I protect them from distractions and obstacles, and they work their butts off for me as a result."

Jan added, "And they don't quit when things get tough. My people are extremely loyal."

Kathryn just listened, but Nick sensed that she was about to offer a counterpoint. "Are you saying that this is a problem? I would think that you would want us to be good managers."

"Of course I do." Kathryn assured them all. "I'm glad to hear how strongly you feel about your staffs. And it's very consistent with what I learned during my initial interviews."

The room waited, as if to say, *So what's the problem?*

Kathryn continued, "But when a company has a collection of good managers who don't act like a team, it can create a dilemma for them, and for the company. You see, it leads to confusion about who their first team is."

Jeff asked for clarification. "First team?"

"Yes, your first team. And all of this relates to the last dysfunction—putting team results ahead of individual issues. Your first team has to be this one." She looked around the room to make it clear that she was referring to the executive staff.

"As strongly as we feel about our own people and as wonderful as that is for them, it simply cannot come at the expense of the loyalty and commitment we have to the group of people sitting here today."

The team digested her remarks, and the difficulty that they implied.

Jan spoke first. "This is a tough one, Kathryn. I mean, it would be easy for me to sit here and agree with you and give you a half-hearted assurance that this would be my first team, but I just don't see how I can abandon what I've worked so hard to build in my department."

Carlos tried to find a happy medium. "I don't think you

have to abandon it." He looked to Kathryn for confirmation.

She squinted, as if dreading having to hold the line. "Well, you don't have to destroy it. But you do have to be willing to make it secondary. And for many of you, that might very well feel like abandonment."

Somewhat discouraged, the group considered the difficult proposition.

Jeff tried to lighten the mood. "Think how crappy this has been for me. You guys *were* my first team. I didn't have anyone else to go to and complain." Everyone, including Mikey, laughed. As much as Jeff was joking, they could see that there was a kernel of truth to what he said, and they felt sorry for him.

Kathryn felt the need to drive a point home. "I don't know how else to say this, but building a team is hard."

No one spoke. Kathryn could see doubt on their faces. But she wasn't deterred by it, because it didn't seem to be about whether building the team was important, but rather whether they could actually do it. Kathryn always preferred that kind of doubt.

PLOWING ON

Kathryn pushed forward. "Listen. We aren't going to solve this one right here. It's a process, and we don't need to get bogged down contemplating our navels for more than a few minutes. Let's just stick to our plan of building a team, and then the prospect of putting this one first might not seem so daunting."

The group seemed ready to shake off their funk, so Kathryn asked a simple question to get things going. "How are we doing?"

Jeff spoke first. "I think we can't deny what has happened since last off-site. I mean, if you would have told me that JR would quit and that we would already have someone like Nick in his place, I would have accused you of engineering the whole thing from the beginning."

Nick agreed. "Well, I never thought I'd be doing this job, and I certainly never thought I'd be having fun at it. But I think we may be in pretty good shape. Still, we have a long way to go to make our numbers."

Kathryn refocused the discussion. "But how are we working as a team?"

Jan replied, "I think we're doing okay. We seem to be moving in the right direction and definitely having more productive conflict."

The group laughed.

"I don't know. I'm starting to have my doubts." Kathryn wouldn't have usually been surprised by a remark like that at this point in the process. Except that it came from Carlos.

"Why is that?" she asked.

Carlos frowned. "I don't know. I guess I still feel like we're not always talking about the big issues. Maybe I'm just getting impatient."

"What big issues are you thinking about?" Jan wondered out loud.

"Well, I don't want to stir things up here . . ."

Kathryn interrupted. "I want you to."

Carlos smiled. "Well, I guess I wonder whether we have our resources in the right place to make this work."

Martin seemed to sense that he was the target of Carlos's remark. And he was right. "What do you mean by resources?"

Carlos stammered, "Well, I don't know. I guess we have a pretty big engineering organization. Almost a third of the company, I think. And, well, we could probably use more resources in sales, marketing, and consulting."

Martin didn't attack statements like that with emotion. He preferred what he liked to call a Sarcratic approach— a sarcastic version of the Socratic method. He was about to challenge Carlos's remark cleverly, until Mikey joined in. "I agree with Carlos. Frankly, I don't know what half our engineers do. And I salivate over the thought of using our money for better marketing and advertising."

Martin sighed audibly as if to say, *Here we go again.* His disgust was not lost on anyone in the room.

Kathryn set the tone for what was about to happen. "Okay, let's have this out. And let's not pretend we're doing anything wrong. We owe it to our shareholders, and our employees, to figure out the right way to use our money. This is not a religious battle. It's about strategy."

Having defused the tension just a bit, Kathryn then stoked the flame. She directed her statement at Martin. "I'm guessing you're tired of people questioning our investment in engineering."

Martin was calm, but intense. "You're damn right I am. What people can't seem to understand is that it's not engineering we're investing in—it's the technology. We are a product company. It's not like I'm spending money taking engineers on golfing trips."

"Come on, Martin," exclaimed Nick. "Engineers don't golf." After lightening the moment with humor, the new head of sales then resumed the conversation. "It's not that we're saying you aren't being personally responsible. It's that you might be a little biased."

Martin was not ready to relent. "Biased? Listen, I go on as many sales calls as anyone else around here. And I speak to analysts . . ."

Jan jumped in now. "Hold on, Martin. We're not questioning your commitment to the company. It's just that you know more about engineering than anything else, and maybe that makes you want to invest in the product." Jan finally went to the heart of the matter. "Why do you get so defensive when someone makes a comment about engineering?"

It was as though Jan had thrown a bucket of cold water on Martin, spilling a little on everyone else in the room.

Mikey piled on, but more gently than usual. "She's right. You act like we're questioning your intelligence."

More calmly now, Martin persisted. "Isn't that what you're doing? You're saying that I'm overestimating the amount of resources it takes to build and maintain our product."

Jan explained with more tact than Mikey could. "No. It's broader than that, Martin. We're questioning how good our products need to be for us to win in the market. We're questioning how much effort we need to be putting behind future technology, because that might come at the expense of having the market embrace our current technology."

Kathryn stepped out of her facilitating role and added to Jan's perspective. "And there is no way that you could figure that out on your own. I don't think anyone here is smart enough, and has the breadth and depth of knowledge, to know the right answer without hearing from everyone else and benefiting from their perspective."

Ironically, the more reasonable the explanation was, the more wound up Martin seemed to become. It was as though he could easily deflect the insecure rants of Mikey, but was being trapped by the fairness and logic of Jan and Kathryn.

"Listen, after all the time we've put into building this product, I am not willing to read a bloody epitaph of our company that blames our demise on bad technology." Before anyone could point out to him that this was a blatant demonstration of the fifth dysfunction, Martin beat them to it. "And yes, I know that sounds a lot like I'm more interested in avoiding individual blame than I am in helping the company win, but . . ." He didn't seem to have a good explanation for his behavior.

Jan bailed him out. "Why do you think I'm so anal about finances?" It was a rhetorical question, so she answered it for everyone. "The last thing I want to do is read in *The Wall Street Journal* that we didn't manage our cash and had to close the company down. And Carlos doesn't want customer support issues to sink us, and Mikey doesn't want us to fail because we can't build our brand."

Even with such an even distribution of blame, Mikey couldn't seem to accept her own portion. She gave Jan a look that said, *I'm not worried about that.*

Jan ignored her and commented to the rest of the group, "It sounds like we're all scrambling for lifeboats on the *Titanic.*"

143

"I don't think it's quite that desperate," countered Nick. Kathryn qualified her CFO's metaphor. "Well, then we're all trying to stand as close to them as possible just in case."

Nick nodded as if to say, *Okay, I'll give you that.* Kathryn put the conversation back on topic and directed her leading question toward Martin. "So where were we?"

Martin took a deep breath, shook his head as if he were disagreeing with everything that had been said, and then surprised everyone. "Okay, let's figure this out."

He went to the white board and mapped out his entire organization, explaining what everyone was working on and how it fit together. His peers were genuinely amazed, both by how much they didn't know about everything going on in engineering and how it all fit together.

After Martin had finished, Kathryn gave the group two hours to discuss the relative merits of expanding or reducing the resources allocated to engineering and how to use them in other areas. During that time, the team argued vehemently at times, changed their minds, retrenched on their original opinions, and then decided that the right answer was not so apparent after all.

Perhaps most important of all, every member of the team, including Kathryn, at one time picked up the marker and went to the white board to explain a point. If anyone yawned, it was because they were exhausted, not bored.

Finally, it was Jeff who offered a solution. He proposed cutting one future product line entirely and delaying another for at least six months. Nick then suggested redeploying the engineers from those projects and training them to assist sales reps with product demonstrations.

Within minutes, the group had agreed, laid out an aggressive time line for implementing the change, and stared in amazement at the complex but workable solution on the white board in front of them.

Kathryn then suggested they go to lunch and added, "When we get back, we're going to be talking about dealing with interpersonal discomfort and holding each other accountable."

"I can't wait." Martin's facetious remark was not intended to be an indictment of the process, and no one took it that way.

ACCOUNTABILITY

After lunch, Kathryn was determined to maintain the momentum of the morning's session, and she decided that focusing on real issues, rather than exercises, was her best bet.

So she asked Nick to lead the team in a review of their progress around their eighteen-deal goal. He went to the board and wrote the four key drivers that the group had agreed to focus on during the previous off-site: product demonstrations, competitive analysis, sales training, and product brochures. Nick went right down the list.

"Okay, Martin, how are you doing with the product demo project?"

"We're ahead of schedule. It turns out to be a little easier than we thought, so we should be done a week or two early. Carlos has been a big help."

Nick didn't like to waste time. "Great. How about competitor analysis? Carlos?"

Carlos looked through a stack of papers on the table in front of him. "I brought an update summary, but I can't find it." He gave up looking. "Anyway, we haven't really started yet. I haven't been able to pull together a meeting."

"Why not?" Nick was more patient than Kathryn expected.

"Well, quite frankly, because many of your people haven't been available. And I've been busy helping Martin with the demo."

Silence.

Nick decided to be constructive. "Okay, which of my people haven't been available?"

Carlos didn't want to point fingers. "I'm not complaining about them. It's just that . . ."

Nick interrupted him. "It's okay, Carlos. Just tell me who needs to be more responsive."

"Well, I think that Jack is key. And Ken. And I'm not sure if . . ."

Now Kathryn interrupted. "Does anyone see a problem here?"

Nick answered first. "Yeah, I need to communicate with my staff about our priorities and make sure they're ready to support them."

Kathryn acknowledged that this was true, but she was looking for something else. "But what about Carlos? Don't you think he should have come to you about fixing this problem before today? Not one of you challenged him when he said he hadn't even started the competitor analysis."

Uncomfortable silence again.

Carlos was secure enough not to overreact to his boss's

question. For the moment, he seemed to be considering it objectively.

Martin jumped in. "It's hard to come down on someone who is always pitching in."

Kathryn nodded and then added firmly. "You're right. But that's not a good excuse. The fact is, Carlos is a vice president of the company, and he needs to prioritize better according to what we agreed to do, and he needs to challenge people in the organization who are not responding to his requests."

Sensing now that Carlos was beginning to feel picked on, Kathryn addressed him directly. "I'm using you as an example, Carlos, because you are an easy person to let off the hook. But this could apply to anyone. Some people are hard to hold accountable because they are so helpful. Others because they get defensive. Others because they are intimidating. I don't think it's easy to hold anyone accountable, not even your own kids."

That brought a few nods of acknowledgment from some of the team members. Kathryn continued, "I want all of you challenging each other about what you are doing, how you are spending your time, whether you are making enough progress."

Mikey challenged, "But that sounds like a lack of trust."

Kathryn shook her head. "No, trust is not the same as assuming everyone is on the same page as you, and that they don't need to be pushed. Trust is knowing that when a team member does push you, they're doing it because they care about the team."

Nick clarified. "But we have to push in a way that doesn't piss people off."

His statement sounded like a question, so Kathryn responded. "Absolutely. Push with respect, and under the assumption that the other person is probably doing the right thing. But push anyway. And never hold back."

The team seemed to be digesting the point well, and Kathryn let it sink in for a moment. Then she asked Nick to continue.

He gladly obliged. "Okay, we're on item number three, which is the sales training program. I own that one myself, and we're on pace. I've scheduled a two-day training session for our salespeople, and I think that all of us should be there too."

Mikey seemed incredulous. "Why?"

"Because we should all consider ourselves to be salespeople. Especially if closing those eighteen deals is really our top priority."

Kathryn left no doubt. "It is."

Nick continued. "Then we are all going to be involved, and we need to know how to help our sales reps." Nick gave everyone the date of the training, and they wrote it in their calendars.

Mikey still seemed peeved.

"Is there a problem, Mikey?" It was Nick who asked.

"No, no. Go ahead."

Nick wouldn't accept that. Containing any frustration that he might have felt, he pushed on. "No, if you think there is a good reason for you not to be at sales training, then I'm open to hearing it." He paused to see if she would respond, and when she didn't, he continued. "Frankly, I can't imagine anything else being more important."

Finally, Mikey responded sarcastically. "Okay, and I'd like everyone to attend next week's product marketing meeting."

Nick restrained himself again. "Really? Because if you think we should all be there, and it makes sense, then we'll do it."

Mikey didn't even consider his offer. "Forget it. I'll be at the sales training. I don't need any of you, other than Martin, at the product marketing meeting."

Right at that moment Kathryn became certain that Mikey would have to go. Unfortunately, the next five minutes would make that harder than she would have liked.

INDIVIDUAL
CONTRIBUTOR

ick moved to the fourth item on the list. "Okay, how are we doing with product brochures?" He directed the question at Mikey.

"We're all set." Mikey's attempt to avoid being smug was transparent.

Nick was a little surprised. "Really?"

Sensing that her peers didn't quite believe her, Mikey reached down into her computer bag, retrieved a stack of glossy leaflets, and began passing them around the room. "This is scheduled to go to print next week."

The room was quiet as everyone scrutinized the design and read the copy. Kathryn could sense that most of them were pleased by the quality of the material.

But Nick seemed uncomfortable. "Were you going to talk to me about this? Because some of the salespeople are out doing customer research for these brochures, and they're going to be a little miffed when they find out that their input was not . . ."

Mikey interrupted. "My staff knows this stuff better than anyone else in the company. But if you want to have someone in your department add their two cents, that would be fine." It was clear that she didn't think it should be necessary.

Nick seemed torn between being impressed by what he was looking at and insulted by the way it was being presented to him. "Okay, I'll send you a list of three or four people who should see this before we go forward."

Any excitement about the progress Mikey had made was blunted by her reaction to Nick.

Jeff tried to make the awkward situation better. "Well, in any case, you and your staff did a great job with this."

Mikey enjoyed the compliment a little too much. "Well, I've been working hard on it. And it's what I do best."

The entire room seemed to groan silently at their colleague's continued lack of humility.

In a rare moment of impulsiveness, Kathryn decided that she could not wait any longer. After announcing that there would be a long afternoon break until dinner at six o'clock, she dismissed everyone. Except Mikey.

THE TALK

As soon as everyone had left the room and the door behind them had closed, Kathryn felt a sense of remorse and a desire to go for a long walk by herself. *How can I get out of this?* she wondered, knowing that there was no backing out now.

Mikey seemed to have no idea what was about to happen. Kathryn couldn't decide if her ignorance would make this easier or harder. She would find out soon enough.

"This is going to be a tough conversation, Mikey."

The marketing vice president briefly flashed a look of realization, and then covered it immediately. "It is?"

Kathryn took a deep breath and went right to the bone. "I don't think you are a fit for this team. And I don't think you really want to be here. Do you know where I'm coming from?"

A genuine sense of shock hit Mikey, which caught Kathryn off guard. *She had to see this coming,* Kathryn moaned to herself.

Mikey was incredulous. "Me? You've got to be kidding. Of all the people on this team, you think that I . . ." She didn't complete the thought, but stared intently at Kathryn. "Me?"

Strangely enough, Kathryn was suddenly more comfortable now that the issue was out on the table. She had dealt with enough obliviously difficult executives in her career to stand firm in the midst of their shock. But Mikey was cleverer than the average executive.

"What's the basis for this?" Mikey demanded.

Calmly, Kathryn explained. "Mikey, you don't seem to respect your colleagues. You aren't willing to open up to them. During meetings, you have an extremely distracting and demotivating impact on all of them. Including me."

As much as Kathryn knew that what she said was true, she was suddenly aware of how shallow her accusations might have sounded to someone unfamiliar with the situation.

"You don't think I respect my colleagues? The problem is that they don't respect me." As the words came out of her mouth, Mikey seemed to realize the gravity of her accidental self-indictment. Slightly frazzled, she tried to clarify. "They don't appreciate the expertise I have. Or my experience. And they certainly don't understand how to market software."

Kathryn listened silently, growing more confident in her decision with every word that Mikey spoke.

Sensing this, Mikey attacked, more calmly but with undeniable venom. "Kathryn, how do you think the board is going to react to my leaving the team? In less than a month, you'll have lost your head of sales and marketing. I'd be pretty worried about my job if I were you."

"I appreciate your concern, Mikey." Kathryn's response had just a touch of sarcasm. "But my job is not to avoid confrontation with the board. My job is to build an executive team that can make this company work." She shifted toward a more compassionate tone. "And I just don't think you like being part of this one."

Mikey now took a breath. "Do you really think that taking me off the team is going to help this company?"

Kathryn nodded. "Yes I do. And I honestly believe it will be better for you too."

"How do you figure that?"

Kathryn decided to be as truthful, and kind, as possible. "Well, you might find a company that appreciates your skills and style more." Kathryn wanted to hold back the next sentence, but realized it was in Mikey's best interest to hear it. "But I think that might not be easy if you don't take a look at yourself."

"What does that mean?"

"It means you seem bitter, Mikey. And maybe that's a DecisionTech thing . . ."

Mikey interrupted before Kathryn could go any further. "It is definitely a DecisionTech thing, because I've never had problems like this before."

Kathryn was sure this wasn't true, but she decided not to rub salt in her wounds. "Then you will definitely be happier somewhere else."

Mikey stared at the table in front of her. Kathryn sensed that she was coming to terms with the situation, even accepting it. She was wrong.

LAST STAND

ikey excused herself to collect her thoughts. When she returned a few minutes later, she seemed more emotional and determined than ever.

"Okay, first of all, I'm not resigning. You'll have to fire me. And my husband is a lawyer, and so I don't think you'll have an easy time making a case against me."

Kathryn didn't flinch. But with complete sincerity and sympathy, she responded. "I'm not firing you. And you don't have to leave."

Mikey seemed confused.

Kathryn clarified the situation. "But your behavior would have to change completely. And it would have to change fast." Kathryn paused to let Mikey consider what she was saying. "And frankly, I'm just not sure that you want to go through that."

The look on Mikey's face indicated that she definitely didn't want to go through that. But she defended herself nonetheless. "I don't think my behavior is the problem around here."

Kathryn responded. "It's certainly not the only one, but it's a very real issue. You don't participate in areas outside your department. You don't accept criticism from your peers, or apologize when you're out of line."

"When have I been out of line?" Mikey demanded to know.

Kathryn couldn't decide whether Mikey was being coy, or if she were truly that socially unaware. In either case, she would have to come clean with her, but calmly. "I don't know where to start. There's the constant rolling of your eyes. There's the rude and disrespectful remarks, like telling Martin he's an s.o.b. There's your lack of interest in attending sales training, even though that's the company's top priority. I would say all of those are pretty out of line."

Mikey sat in stunned silence. Confronted with such stark evidence, she suddenly seemed to realize the weight of her dilemma. Still, she had a few rounds of ammunition left before she would cede defeat. "Listen, I'm sick of hearing people complain about me. And I'm certainly not going to change in order to fit in with this dysfunctional group of people. But I'm not just going to make this easy for you and leave. This is about principle."

Kathryn remained confident. "What principle?"

Mikey couldn't come up with a specific answer. She just looked at Kathryn coldly, shaking her head.

Almost a full minute passed. Kathryn resisted breaking the silence, wanting Mikey to sit with herself and see the emptiness of her arguments. Finally, Mikey said, "I want three months' severance, all my stock options vested, and the official record to show that I resigned on my own accord."

Relieved, Kathryn was more than happy to give Mikey everything she asked for. But she knew better than to say so right there. "I'm not sure about all of that, but I'll see if I can make it happen."

A few more awkward moments of silence passed. "So, do you just want me to leave right now? I mean, should I not even stay for dinner?"

Kathryn nodded. "You can come get your things at the office next week. And meet with HR to work out your exit package, assuming I can get you what you want."

"You know you guys are screwed, don't you?" Mikey was going to punish Kathryn one way or another. "I mean, you have no sales or marketing people left. And I wouldn't be surprised if you lost some of my staff members as a result of this."

But Kathryn had been through this kind of situation plenty of times before, and she'd spent enough time with Mikey's staff to know they saw many of the same flaws in their boss that everyone else did. Still, she felt it would be best to demonstrate some degree of concern. "Well, I would certainly understand if that happened, but I hope it's not the case."

Mikey shook her head again, as though she were about to launch into another tirade. And then she picked up her computer bag and left.

FLACK

Kathryn spent the rest of the break taking a long walk around the vineyards. When the meeting resumed, she was refreshed—but completely unprepared for what was about to happen.

Before Kathryn could raise the subject, Nick asked, "Where's Mikey?"

Kathryn wanted to deliver the message without seeming too relieved. "Mikey isn't going to be coming back. She's leaving the company."

The looks on the faces of the people around the table didn't seem to fit Kathryn's expectations. They appeared to be surprised.

"How did that happen?" Jan wanted to know.

"Well, what I'm about to say needs to be confidential because of legal issues relating to departed employees." Everyone nodded.

Kathryn was direct. "I didn't see Mikey being willing to

adjust her behavior. And it was hurting the team. So I asked her to leave the company."

No one spoke. They just looked at one another and at the brochures still sitting on the table in front of them.

Finally, Carlos spoke. "Wow. I don't know what to say. How did she take it? What are we going to do about marketing?"

Nick continued the list of questions. "What are we going to say to employees? To the press?"

As surprised as Kathryn was by their response, she quickly summoned an answer. "I don't want to say a lot about how Mikey responded. She was a little surprised, a little angry, neither of which is rare in situations like this."

The group waited for Kathryn to address the other issues.

She continued. "And as far as what we're going to do about marketing, we'll start looking for a new vice president. But we've got plenty of strong people in the organization now who can step up and keep things moving until then. I have no concerns about that."

Everyone seemed to digest and agree with Kathryn's explanation.

"And we'll have to simply tell employees and the press that Mikey is moving on. We don't have a lot of flexibility there, in terms of getting into sensitive information. But I don't think we should be intimidated by anyone's initial reactions. If we get our act together and make progress, employees and analysts alike are going to be fine. And I think most people, especially employees, won't be all that surprised."

As confident as Kathryn was and as logical as her reasoning seemed, the mood in the room remained down. Kathryn knew she would have to push them hard to focus on real work. She didn't realize how much more work she had to do to put the Mikey issue to rest.

HEAVY LIFTING

For the rest of the evening and into the next afternoon, the group focused on the details of the business, with special attention on sales. Though they certainly made progress, Kathryn could not deny that Mikey's departure was continuing to dampen the general atmosphere. She decided to enter the danger.

When lunch was over, Kathryn addressed the group. "I'd like to take a few minutes to deal with the elephant that's sitting in the corner. I want to know how everyone is feeling about Mikey leaving. Because we need to make sure that we deal with this as a team before I stand in front of the company and explain it to them next week." Though it always amazed her, Kathryn knew from past experience that the departure of even the most difficult employees provoked some degree of mourning and self-doubt among their peers.

Team members looked around at one another to see who would go first. It was Nick. "I guess I'm just worried about losing another member of the executive team."

Kathryn nodded to acknowledge his concern but really wanted to say, *But she was never a member of this team!*

Jan added, "I know she was a difficult person, but the quality of her work was good. And marketing is critical right now. Maybe we should have just tolerated her."

Kathryn nodded to indicate that she was listening. "Anyone else?"

Martin sort of raised his hand, making it clear that he was about to make a statement that he didn't want to make. "I guess I'm just wondering who's next."

Kathryn paused before responding. "Let me tell you a quick story about myself. One that I'm not too proud of."

That got everyone's attention.

Kathryn frowned, as if she didn't really want to do what she was about to do. "While I was in my last quarter of graduate school, I took a job as a contractor at a well-known retail company in San Francisco, where I ran a small department of financial analysts. It was my first real management position, and I was hoping to land a permanent job with the company after graduation."

In spite of her limitations as a public speaker, Kathryn had a knack for telling stories. "I inherited a pretty good group of people. They all worked hard, but one guy in particular cranked out more reports, and better ones, than anyone else. I'll call him Fred. Fred took any assignment I gave him and became my most reliable employee."

"Sounds like a problem I'd like to have," Nick commented.

Kathryn raised her eyebrows. "Well, there's more to the story. No one else in the department could stand Fred. And to be honest, he annoyed the heck out of me too. He didn't help anyone with their work, and he made sure everyone knew how much better he was at his job, which was undeniable, even to the people who hated the guy. Anyway, my staff came to me a number of times complaining about Fred. I listened carefully and even spoke to Fred half-heartedly about adjusting his behavior. But I mostly ignored them because I could tell that they resented his skills. More importantly, I was not about to come down on my top performer."

The staff seemed to empathize with her.

Kathryn went on. "Eventually, the output of the department began to slide, and so I gave more work to Fred, who complained a little but managed to get it all done. In my mind, he was carrying the department. Pretty soon, morale in the department began to deteriorate more rapidly than ever, and our performance slid further. Again, a number of analysts came to me to complain about Fred, and it was becoming clear that he was indeed contributing to the problems of the group more than I had thought. After a tough night of thinking and losing sleep, I made my first big decision."

Jeff guessed, "You fired him."

Kathryn smiled in a shameful kind of way. "No. I promoted him."

Jaws around the table dropped.

Kathryn nodded her head. "That's right. Fred was my first promotion as a manager. Two weeks later, three of my seven analysts quit, and the department fell into chaos. We dropped way behind in our work, and my manager called me in to talk about what was going on. I explained the Fred situation, and why I had lost the other analysts. The next day, he made a big decision."

Jeff guessed again. "He fired him."

Kathryn smiled in a painfully humorous way. "Close. He fired *me.*"

The staff seemed surprised. Jan wanted to make her feel better. "But companies don't usually fire contractors."

Kathryn was suddenly a little sarcastic. "Okay. Let's just say that the assignment ended abruptly, and they never bothered to have me back."

Nick and Martin smiled, trying not to crack up. Kathryn completed their thoughts. "I definitely got fired."

Everyone in the room laughed.

"What happened to Fred?" Jeff wanted to know.

"I hear that he quit a few weeks later, and they hired someone else to run the department. Performance improved dramatically within a month of his departure, even though the department now had three fewer analysts than before."

"Are you saying that Fred's behavior alone hurt the production of the group by 50 percent?"

"No. Not Fred's behavior."

People seemed confused.

"My tolerance of his behavior. Listen, they fired the right person."

No one spoke. They seemed to be feeling their boss's pain, and making the obvious connection between Kathryn's story and what had happened the day before.

After a few moments, Kathryn brought her lesson home. "I don't plan on losing any of you. And that's why I did what I did."

At that moment, everyone in the room seemed to understand her.

RALLY

B
ack at the office, Kathryn held an all-hands meeting to discuss Mikey's departure and other company issues. In spite of her typically tactful and gracious demeanor, the news provoked more concern among employees than the executives had expected. And though they agreed that the reaction had more to do with its symbolic meaning than with losing Mikey in particular, it dampened the enthusiasm of the team.

So during the next staff meeting, Kathryn had the group spend more than an hour discussing how they were going to replace their head of marketing. After a heated debate about whether to promote one of Mikey's direct reports, Kathryn stepped in to break the tie.

"All right. This has been a good discussion, and I think I've heard everyone. Does anyone have anything else to add?"

No one spoke, so Kathryn continued. "I believe that we need to find someone who can grow the department and help us with branding. And as much as I would prefer to promote someone internally, I don't see anyone in the department who is close to being able to do that right now.

And so I think we should begin a search for a new vice president."

Every head in the room nodded support, even those who had argued against an outside hire.

"But I can assure you that we're going to find the right person. That means everyone here will be interviewing candidates and pushing to find someone who can demonstrate trust, engage in conflict, commit to group decisions, hold their peers accountable, and focus on the results of the team, not their own ego."

Kathryn was certain that her staff had begun to buy in to her theory. After asking Jeff to organize the search for the new VP, she shifted the topic to sales.

Nick reported that progress had been made with a few key prospects, and that some regions of the country were still struggling. "I think we need more feet on the street."

Jan knew that Nick was asking for more money and tried to put a quick halt to his thinking. "I don't want to add more expenses because that only means your quotas will go up. We don't want to get into a death spiral here."

Nick breathed hard and shook his head in exasperation as if to say, *There you go again.* Before anyone knew what was going on, Nick and Jan were pounding on the table trying to convince one another, and the rest of the group, that their approach was right.

During a brief pause in the action, Jan threw herself back in her chair in frustration and proclaimed, "Nothing around here has changed. Maybe the problem wasn't Mikey after all."

That sobered the group.

Kathryn jumped in, smiling. "Hold on. Hold on. I don't see anything wrong here. This is the kind of conflict we've been talking about for the past month. It's perfect."

Jan tried to explain herself. "I guess I just don't see it that way. It still feels like we're fighting."

"You *are* fighting. But about issues. That's your job. Otherwise, you leave it to your people to try to solve problems that they can't solve. They want you to hash this stuff out so they can get clear direction from us."

Jan seemed tired. "I hope this is worth it."

Kathryn smiled again. "Trust me. It will be worth it in more ways than you know."

Over the next two weeks, Kathryn began to push her team harder than ever before around their behavior. She chided Martin for eroding trust by appearing smug during meetings. She forced Carlos to confront the team about their lack of responsiveness to customer issues. And she spent more than one late night with Jan and Nick, working through budget battles that had to be fought.

More important than what Kathryn did, however, was the reaction she received. As resistant as they might have seemed in the moment, no one questioned whether they should be doing the things that Kathryn made them do. There seemed to be a genuine sense of collective purpose.

The only question that remained in Kathryn's mind was whether she could keep it going long enough for everyone to see the benefits.

PART FOUR

Traction

HARVEST

lthough the last of Kathryn's Napa Valley off-sites had a different atmosphere from the others, it began with a familiar speech. "We have a more experienced set of executives than any of our competitors. We have more cash than they do. Thanks to Martin and his team, we have better core technology. And we have a more connected board of directors. Yet in spite of all that, we are behind two of our competitors in terms of both revenue and customer growth. And I think we all know why that is."

Nick raised his hand. "Kathryn, I'd like you to stop giving that speech."

A month earlier, everyone in the room would have been shocked by such a blunt statement. But no one seemed to be alarmed at all.

"Why is that?" Kathryn asked.

Nick frowned, trying to think of the right words. "I guess it seemed more appropriate a few weeks ago when we were a lot more . . ." Nick didn't need to finish the sentence.

Kathryn explained as nicely as she could. "I'll stop making this speech when it's no longer true. We are still behind two of our competitors. And we are still not where we need to be as a team."

Kathryn continued. "But that's not to say that we aren't on the right track. In fact, the first thing we're going to do today is take a step back and assess where we are as a team."

Kathryn went to the white board and drew the triangle again, filling in the five dysfunctions.

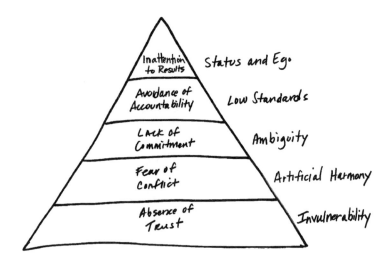

Then she asked, "How are we doing?"

The team considered the question as they re-examined the model.

Finally, Jeff spoke first. "We certainly trust each other more than we did a month ago." Heads around the room nodded, and Jeff completed the thought. "Although I think that it's still too early to say that there isn't more work to be done." Heads continued to nod.

Jan added. "And we're doing better with conflict, although I can't say I'm used to it yet."

Kathryn assured her, "I don't think anyone ever gets completely used to conflict. If it's not a little uncomfortable, then it's not real. The key is to keep doing it anyway."

Jan accepted the explanation.

Nick jumped in. "As far as commitment is concerned, we have definitely started getting better buy-in around objectives and deliverables. That's not a problem. But the next one, accountability, worries me the most."

"Why?" asked Jeff.

"Because I'm not sure that we're going to be willing to get in each other's faces when someone doesn't deliver, or if someone starts acting against the good of the team."

"*I'm* certainly going to get in their face."

To everyone's surprise, it was Martin who made the comment. He explained. "I don't think I could handle going back to the way things were before. And so if it comes down to a little interpersonal discomfort versus politics, I'm opting for the discomfort."

Nick smiled at his quirky colleague and finished the model. "Well, I don't think we're going to have a results problem. None of us will come out of this smelling rosy if we can't make this company work."

Kathryn had never been so glad to see a room full of people nod their heads in agreement. But she decided that she should let some of the air out of the team's balloon.

"Listen, I agree with most of what you've said about the team. You're moving in the right direction. But I want to assure you that there will be many days during the next few months when you will wonder if you've made any progress at all. It's going to take more than a few weeks of behavioral change before we see a tangible impact on the bottom line."

The team seemed to be agreeing with her too easily. She decided she needed to rattle them one more time. "I'm telling you this because we are not out of the woods yet. I've seen plenty of groups slide backward that were a lot further along than we are. This is about having the discipline and persistence to keep doing what we're doing."

As bad as Kathryn felt about raining on the team's parade, she was relieved to have prepared them for the bad weather every team faces on the way to shedding their dysfunctions. And for the next two days, the team experienced that weather. At times, working together in a spirit of cooperation, at other times seemingly at each other's throats, the group wrestled with business issues and worked each one through to resolution. Ironically, they rarely discussed the notion of teamwork directly, which Kathryn interpreted as a sign that they were making progress. Two observations that Kathryn made during breaks and meals told her she was right.

First, the team seemed to stay together, choosing not to go off on their own as they had at previous off-sites. Second, they were noisier than they had ever been, and one of the most prevalent sounds that could be heard among them was laughter. By the end of the session, though they were clearly exhausted, everyone seemed eager to schedule follow-up meetings with one another when they returned to the office.

GUT CHECK

Three months after the final off-site had ended, Kathryn held her first quarterly two-day staff meeting at a local hotel. The new vice president of marketing, Joseph Charles, had joined DecisionTech a week earlier and was attending his first meeting with the group.

Kathryn kicked off the session by making an announcement that no one was prepared for. "Remember Green Banana? The company that we considered buying last quarter?"

Heads around the table nodded.

"Well, evidently Nick was right about their being a possible competitor. They want to buy us."

Everyone except Jeff, who sat on the board and already knew about the offer, was shocked. No one more so than Nick. "I thought they were in financial trouble?"

"They were," explained Kathryn. "I guess they raised a truckload of money last month and are suddenly hungry to buy something. They've already made us an offer."

"What's it look like?" Jan wanted to know.

Kathryn looked at her notes. "Quite a bit more than our estimated worth today. We would all make decent money."

Jan pressed on. "What did the board say?"

Jeff answered for Kathryn. "They're leaving it up to us."

No one spoke. It was as if they were all calculating their potential payouts and trying to put the offer into some sort of context.

Finally, an almost angry voice with a British accent broke the silence. "No bloody way."

Everyone turned toward their head of engineering. He spoke with more passion than anyone had ever heard from him. "There is no way that I am going to walk away from all of this and hand it over to a company named after a piece of unripened fruit."

The group burst out into laughter.

Jan brought them back down to earth. "I don't think we should discard this quite so fast. There is no guarantee that we're going to make it. This is real money."

Jeff added to his CFO's point. "The board certainly doesn't think it's a bad offer."

Martin didn't seem to believe Jeff. "Then why did they leave it to us to make the decision?"

Jeff paused for a moment before explaining. "Because they want to know that we have the fire in our bellies."

Martin frowned. "The what?"

Jeff clarified for his British colleague. "They want to know if we want to be here. If we're really committed to the company. And to each other."

Joseph summarized the situation. "It sounds like this is a gut check."

Carlos spoke for the first time during the meeting. "I vote against it."

Jeff was next. "So do I. Definitely."

Nick nodded his head. As did Kathryn and Joseph.

Martin looked at Jan. "What do you say?"

She hesitated for a moment. "Green Banana? Are you kidding?"

They broke into laughter.

Kathryn quickly refocused the meeting, wanting to capture the momentum and direct it toward real business. "Okay, we've got plenty of other big topics to take care of today. So let's get started."

For the next several hours, the group took Joseph through the five dysfunctions. Nick explained the importance of trust. Jan and Jeff together covered conflict and commitment. Carlos described accountability within the context of the team, and Martin finished off results. They then reviewed Joseph's Myers-Briggs results and explained the roles and responsibilities of his new peers, as well as their collective goals.

Most importantly, for the rest of the day they launched into some of the most passionate debates Joseph had ever heard and ended those debates with crystal-clear agreements and no sense of lingering bitterness. They called each other on the carpet once or twice in ways that made

Joseph uncomfortable, but in each case they brought the discussions around to results.

By the end of the session, Joseph decided he had joined one of the most unusual and intense executive teams he had ever seen, and he couldn't wait to become an active part of it.

THE MARCH

Over the course of the next year, DecisionTech grew its sales dramatically, and met its revenue goals during three of its four quarters. The company moved into a virtual tie for the number one position in the industry, but had yet to separate itself from its chief rival.

With the substantial improvement in performance, the company saw turnover among employees subside and morale rise steadily, with the exception of a slight and temporary dip when the company missed its numbers.

Interestingly, when that happened, even the Chairman called to encourage Kathryn not to get too disappointed in light of the undeniable progress she had made.

With more than 250 employees, Kathryn decided it was time to trim down the number of executives who reported directly to her. She believed that the larger the company, the smaller the team should be at the top. And with the addition of a new head of sales and a human resources director, her staff had grown to a barely manageable eight. It wasn't that Kathryn couldn't handle the weekly one-on-ones, but it was increasingly difficult to have fluid and substantive discussions during staff meetings with nine people sitting around the table. Even with the new collective attitude of the members of the team, it would be only a matter of time before problems began to surface.

So more than a year after the final Napa off-site had ended, Kathryn decided to make a few organizational changes, which she delicately but confidently explained to each of her staff members. Nick would again assume the role of chief operating officer, a title he finally felt he had earned. Carlos and the new head of sales would report to him and would no longer be on the CEO's staff. Human resources would report to Jan, leaving Kathryn with five direct reports: Martin as CTO, Jan as CFO, Nick as COO, Joseph as VP of marketing, and Jeff as VP of business development.

A week later, another of Kathryn's quarterly two-day staff meetings took place. Before Kathryn could start the meeting, Jan wanted to know, "Where's Jeff?"

Kathryn responded matter-of-factly. "That's what I wanted to talk about first today. Jeff won't be coming to these meetings any more."

The room was stunned. Both at what Kathryn had said, and that she said it with so little emotion.

Finally, Jan asked the question that everyone was thinking. "Jeff quit?"

Kathryn seemed a little surprised by the question. "No."

Martin then followed. "You didn't fire him, did you?"

Suddenly it occurred to Kathryn what everyone was

thinking. "No, of course not. Why would I fire Jeff? It's just that he'll be reporting to Nick from now on. Given his new role, he and I both agree that it makes a lot of sense."

As much as everyone was relieved that their worst fears had been allayed, there was still something bothering them.

Jan couldn't hold back. "Kathryn, I can certainly see that it makes sense. And frankly, I'm sure that Nick is glad to have Jeff on his team."

Nick nodded to confirm this, and Jan continued. "But don't you think he's disappointed about not reporting directly to you anymore? I mean, I know we're not supposed to be concerned with status and ego and all of that, but he is a board member, and a founder. Did you really consider what this means to him?"

Kathryn smiled proudly, delighted that they had forced her to explain what she had been wanting to tell them all along. "You guys, this was Jeff's idea."

That thought had not occurred to any of them. Kathryn went on. "He said that as much as he wanted to stay on the team, it made more sense for him to be part of Nick's group. I actually gave him a chance to change his mind, and he insisted it was the right thing to do for the company, and for the team."

Kathryn let her team enjoy a silent moment of admiration for their former CEO.

And then she continued. "I think we owe it to Jeff and everyone else at this company to make this work. Let's get started."

The Model

AS DIFFICULT as it is to build a cohesive team, it is not complicated. In fact, keeping it simple is critical, whether you run the executive staff at a multinational company, a small department within a larger organization, or even if you are merely a member of a team that needs improvement. In that spirit, this section is designed to provide a clear, concise, and practical guide to using the Five Dysfunctions Model to improve your team. Good luck.

AN OVERVIEW
OF THE MODEL

I n the course of my experience working with CEOs and their teams, two critical truths have become clear to me. First, genuine teamwork in most organizations remains as elusive as it has ever been. Second, organizations fail to achieve teamwork because they unknowingly fall prey to five natural but dangerous pitfalls, which I call the five dysfunctions of a team.

These dysfunctions can be mistakenly interpreted as five distinct issues that can be addressed in isolation of the others. But in reality they form an interrelated model, making susceptibility to even one of them potentially lethal for the success of a team. A cursory overview of each dysfunction, and the model they comprise, should make this clearer.

1. The first dysfunction is an **absence of trust** among team members. Essentially, this stems from their unwillingness to be vulnerable within the group. Team members who are not genuinely open with one another about their mistakes and weaknesses make it impossible to build a foundation for trust.

2. This failure to build trust is damaging because it sets the tone for the second dysfunction: **fear of conflict.** Teams that lack trust are incapable of engaging in unfiltered and passionate debate of ideas. Instead, they resort to veiled discussions and guarded comments.

3. A lack of healthy conflict is a problem because it ensures the third dysfunction of a team: **lack of com-**

mitment. Without having aired their opinions in the course of passionate and open debate, team members rarely, if ever, buy in and commit to decisions, though they may feign agreement during meetings.

4. Because of this lack of real commitment and buy-in, team members develop an **avoidance of accountability,** the fourth dysfunction. Without committing to a clear plan of action, even the most focused and driven people often hesitate to call their peers on actions and behaviors that seem counterproductive to the good of the team.

5. Failure to hold one another accountable creates an environment where the fifth dysfunction can thrive. **Inattention to results** occurs when team members put their individual needs (such as ego, career development, or recognition) or even the needs of their divisions above the collective goals of the team.

And so, like a chain with just one link broken, teamwork deteriorates if even a single dysfunction is allowed to flourish.

Another way to understand this model is to take the opposite approach—a positive one—and imagine how members of truly cohesive teams behave:

1. They trust one another.
2. They engage in unfiltered conflict around ideas.

3. They commit to decisions and plans of action.
4. They hold one another accountable for delivering against those plans.
5. They focus on the achievement of collective results.

If this sounds simple, it's because it is simple, at least in theory. In practice, however, it is extremely difficult because it requires levels of discipline and persistence that few teams can muster.

Before diving into each of the dysfunctions and exploring ways to overcome them, it might be helpful to assess your team and identify where the opportunities for improvement lie in your organization.

TEAM ASSESSMENT

The questionnaire on the following pages is a straightforward diagnostic tool for helping you evaluate your team's susceptibility to the five dysfunctions. At the end of the questionnaire, on page 194, there is a simple explanation of how to tabulate the results and interpret the possible conclusions. If possible, have all members of your team complete the diagnostic and review the results, discussing discrepancies in the responses and identifying any clear implications for the team.

Instructions: Use the scale below to indicate how each statement applies to your team. It is important to evaluate the statements honestly and without over-thinking your answers.

3 = Usually
2 = Sometimes
1 = Rarely

_____ 1. Team members are passionate and unguarded in their discussion of issues.

_____ 2. Team members call out one another's deficiencies or unproductive behaviors.

_____ 3. Team members know what their peers are working on and how they contribute to the collective good of the team.

_____ 4. Team members quickly and genuinely apologize to one another when they say or do something inappropriate or possibly damaging to the team.

_____ 5. Team members willingly make sacrifices (such as budget, turf, head count) in their departments or areas of expertise for the good of the team.

_____ 6. Team members openly admit their weaknesses and mistakes.

_____ 7. Team meetings are compelling, and not boring.

_____ 8. Team members leave meetings confident that their peers are completely committed to the decisions that were agreed on, even if there was initial disagreement.

_____ 9. Morale is significantly affected by the failure to achieve team goals.

_____ 10. During team meetings, the most important—and difficult—issues are put on the table to be resolved.

_____ 11. Team members are deeply concerned about the prospect of letting down their peers.

_____ 12. Team members know about one another's personal lives and are comfortable discussing them.

_____ 13. Team members end discussions with clear and specific resolutions and calls to action.

_____ 14. Team members challenge one another about their plans and approaches.

_____ 15. Team members are slow to seek credit for their own contributions, but quick to point out those of others.

Scoring

Combine your scores for the preceding statements as indicated below.

Dysfunction 1: Absence of Trust	Dysfunction 2: Fear of Conflict	Dysfunction 3: Lack of Commitment	Dysfunction 4: Avoidance of Accountability	Dysfunction 5: Inattention to Results
Statement 4:_____	Statement 1:_____	Statement 3:_____	Statement 2:_____	Statement 5:_____
Statement 6:_____	Statement 7:_____	Statement 8:_____	Statement 11:_____	Statement 9:_____
Statement 12:_____	Statement 10:_____	Statement 13:_____	Statement 14:_____	Statement 15:_____
Total:_____	Total:_____	Total:_____	Total:_____	Total:_____

A score of 8 or 9 is a probable indication that the dysfunction is not a problem for your team.

A score of 6 or 7 indicates that the dysfunction could be a problem.

A score of 3 to 5 is probably an indication that the dysfunction needs to be addressed.

Regardless of your scores, it is important to keep in mind that every team needs constant work, because without it, even the best ones deviate toward dysfunction.

UNDERSTANDING AND OVERCOMING THE FIVE DYSFUNCTIONS

DYSFUNCTION 1: ABSENCE OF TRUST

Trust lies at the heart of a functioning, cohesive team. Without it, teamwork is all but impossible.

Unfortunately, the word *trust* is used—and misused—so often that it has lost some of its impact and begins to sound like motherhood and apple pie. That is why it is important to be very specific about what is meant by trust.

In the context of building a team, trust is the confidence among team members that their peers' intentions are good, and that there is no reason to be protective or careful around the group. In essence, teammates must get comfortable being vulnerable with one another.

This description stands in contrast to a more standard definition of trust, one that centers around the ability to predict a person's behavior based on past experience. For instance, one might "trust" that a given teammate will produce high-quality work because he has always done so in the past.

As desirable as this may be, it is not enough to represent the kind of trust that is characteristic of a great team. It requires team members to make themselves vulnerable to one another, and be confident that their respective vulnerabilities will not be used against them. The vulnerabilities I'm referring to include weaknesses, skill deficiencies, interpersonal shortcomings, mistakes, and requests for help.

As "soft" as all of this might sound, it is only when team members are truly comfortable being exposed to one another that they begin to act without concern for protecting themselves. As a result, they can focus their energy and attention completely on the job at hand, rather than on being strategically disingenuous or political with one another.

Achieving vulnerability-based trust is difficult because in the course of career advancement and education, most successful people learn to be competitive with their peers, and protective of their reputations. It is a challenge for them to turn those instincts off for the good of a team, but that is exactly what is required.

The costs of failing to do this are great. Teams that lack trust waste inordinate amounts of time and energy managing their behaviors and interactions within the group. They tend to dread team meetings, and are reluctant to take risks in asking for or offering assistance to others. As a result, morale on distrusting teams is usually quite low, and unwanted turnover is high.

Members of teams with an absence of trust ...
- Conceal their weaknesses and mistakes from one another
- Hesitate to ask for help or provide constructive feedback
- Hesitate to offer help outside their own areas of responsibility
- Jump to conclusions about the intentions and aptitudes of others without attempting to clarify them
- Fail to recognize and tap into one another's skills and experiences
- Waste time and energy managing their behaviors for effect
- Hold grudges
- Dread meetings and find reasons to avoid spending time together

Members of trusting teams ...
- Admit weaknesses and mistakes
- Ask for help
- Accept questions and input about their areas of responsibility
- Give one another the benefit of the doubt before arriving at a negative conclusion
- Take risks in offering feedback and assistance
- Appreciate and tap into one another's skills and experiences
- Focus time and energy on important issues, not politics
- Offer and accept apologies without hesitation
- Look forward to meetings and other opportunities to work as a group

Suggestions for Overcoming Dysfunction 1

How does a team go about building trust? Unfortunately, vulnerability-based trust cannot be achieved overnight. It requires shared experiences over time, multiple instances of follow-through and credibility, and an in-depth understanding of the unique attributes of team members. However, by taking a focused approach, a team can dramatically accelerate the process and achieve trust in relatively short order. Here are a few tools that can bring this about.

197

Personal Histories Exercise In less than an hour, a team can take the first steps toward developing trust. This low-risk exercise requires nothing more than going around the table during a meeting and having team members answer a short list of questions about themselves. Questions need not be overly sensitive in nature and might include the following: number of siblings, hometown, unique challenges of childhood, favorite hobbies, first job, and worst job. Simply by describing these relatively innocuous attributes or experiences, team members begin to relate to one another on a more personal basis, and see one another as human beings with life stories and interesting backgrounds. This encourages greater empathy and understanding, and discourages unfair and inaccurate behavioral attributions. It is amazing how little some team members know about one another, and how just a small amount of information begins to break down barriers. (Minimum time required: 30 minutes.)

Team Effectiveness Exercise This exercise is more rigorous and relevant than the previous one, but may involve more risk. It requires team members to identify the single most important contribution that each of their peers makes to the team, as well as the one area that they must either improve upon or eliminate for the good of the team. All members then report their responses, focusing on one person at a time, usually beginning with the team leader.

While this exercise may seem somewhat intrusive and

dangerous at first glance, it is remarkable how manageable it can be and how much useful information, both constructive and positive, can be extracted in about an hour. And though the Team Effectiveness Exercise certainly requires some degree of trust in order to be useful, even a relatively dysfunctional team can often make it work with surprisingly little tension. (Minimum time required: 60 minutes.)

Personality and Behavioral Preference Profiles   Some of the most effective and lasting tools for building trust on a team are profiles of team members' behavioral preferences and personality styles. These help break down barriers by allowing people to better understand and empathize with one another.

The best profiling tool, in my opinion, is the Myers-Briggs Type Indicator (MBTI). However, a number of others are popular among different audiences. The purpose of most of these tools is to provide practical and scientifically valid behavioral descriptions of various team members according to the diverse ways that they think, speak, and act. Some of the best characteristics of tools like the MBTI are their nonjudgmental nature (no type is better than another, although they differ substantially), their basis in research (they are not founded upon astrology or new age science), and the extent to which participants take an active role in identifying their own types (they don't simply receive a computer printout or test score that alone dictates their type). Many of these tools do require the participation of a licensed consultant, which is important to avoid the misuse of their powerful implications and applications. (Minimum time required: 4 hours.)

360-Degree Feedback   These tools have become popular over the past twenty years and can produce powerful results for a team. They are riskier than any of the tools or exercises described so far because they call for peers to make specific judgments and provide one another with constructive criticism. The key to making a 360-degree program work, in my opinion, is divorcing it entirely from compensation and formal performance evaluation. Rather, it should be used as a developmental tool, one that allows employees to identify strengths and weaknesses without any repercussions. By being even slightly connected to formal performance evaluation or compensation, 360-degree programs can take on dangerous political undertones.

Experiential Team Exercises   Ropes courses and other experiential team activities seem to have lost some of their luster over the course of the past ten years, and deservedly so. Still, many teams do them with the hope of building trust. And while there are certainly some benefits derived from rigorous and creative outdoor activities involving collective support and cooperation, those benefits do not always translate directly to the working world. That being said, experiential team exercises can be valuable tools for enhancing teamwork as long as they are layered upon more fundamental and relevant processes.

While each of these tools and exercises can have a significant short-term impact on a team's ability to build trust, they must be accompanied by regular follow-up in the course of daily work. Individual developmental areas must be revisited to ensure that progress does not lose momentum. Even on a strong team—and perhaps especially so—atrophy can lead to the erosion of trust.

The Role of the Leader

The most important action that a leader must take to encourage the building of trust on a team is to demonstrate vulnerability first. This requires that a leader risk losing face in front of the team, so that subordinates will take the same risk themselves. What is more, team leaders must create an environment that does not punish vulnerability. Even well-intentioned teams can subtly discourage trust by chastising one another for admissions of weakness or failure. Finally, displays of vulnerability on the part of a team leader must be genuine; they cannot be staged. One of the best ways to lose the trust of a team is to feign vulnerability in order to manipulate the emotions of others.

Connection to Dysfunction 2

How does all of this relate to the next dysfunction, the fear of conflict? By building trust, a team makes conflict possible because team members do not hesitate to engage in passionate and sometimes emotional debate, knowing that they will not be punished for saying something that might otherwise be interpreted as destructive or critical.

DYSFUNCTION 2: FEAR OF CONFLICT

All great relationships, the ones that last over time, require productive conflict in order to grow. This is true in marriage, parenthood, friendship, and certainly business.

Unfortunately, conflict is considered taboo in many situations, especially at work. And the higher you go up the management chain, the more you find people spending inordinate amounts of time and energy trying to avoid the kind of passionate debates that are essential to any great team.

It is important to distinguish productive ideological conflict from destructive fighting and interpersonal politics. Ideological conflict is limited to concepts and ideas, and avoids personality-focused, mean-spirited attacks. However, it can have many of the same external qualities of interpersonal conflict—passion, emotion, and frustration—so much so that an outside observer might easily mistake it for unproductive discord.

But teams that engage in productive conflict know that the only purpose is to produce the best possible solution in the shortest period of time. They discuss and resolve issues more quickly and completely than others, and they emerge from heated debates with no residual feelings or collateral damage, but with an eagerness and readiness to take on the next important issue.

Ironically, teams that avoid ideological conflict often do so in order to avoid hurting team members' feelings, and then end up encouraging dangerous tension. When team members do not openly debate and disagree about important ideas, they often turn to back-channel personal attacks, which are far nastier and more harmful than any heated argument over issues.

It is also ironic that so many people avoid conflict in the name of efficiency, because healthy conflict is actually a time saver. Contrary to the notion that teams waste time and energy arguing, those that avoid conflict actually doom themselves to revisiting issues again and again without resolution. They often ask team members to take their issues "off-line," which seems to be a euphemism for avoiding dealing with an important topic, only to have it raised again at the next meeting.

Suggestions for Overcoming Dysfunction 2

How does a team go about developing the ability and willingness to engage in healthy conflict? The first step is acknowledging that conflict is productive, and that many teams have a tendency to avoid it. As long as some team

Teams that fear conflict ...

- Have boring meetings
- Create environments where back-channel politics and personal attacks thrive
- Ignore controversial topics that are critical to team success
- Fail to tap into all the opinions and perspectives of team members
- Waste time and energy with posturing and interpersonal risk management

Teams that engage in conflict ...

- Have lively, interesting meetings
- Extract and exploit the ideas of all team members
- Solve real problems quickly
- Minimize politics
- Put critical topics on the table for discussion

members believe that conflict is unnecessary, there is little chance that it will occur. But beyond mere recognition, there are a few simple methods for making conflict more common and productive.

Mining   Members of teams that tend to avoid conflict must occasionally assume the role of a "miner of conflict"— someone who extracts buried disagreements within the team and sheds the light of day on them. They must have the courage and confidence to call out sensitive issues and force team members to work through them. This requires a degree of objectivity during meetings and a commitment to staying with the conflict until it is resolved. Some teams may want to assign a member of the team to take on this responsibility during a given meeting or discussion.

Real-Time Permission   In the process of mining for conflict, team members need to coach one another not to retreat from healthy debate. One simple but effective way to do this is to recognize when the people engaged in conflict are becoming uncomfortable with the level of discord, and then interrupt to remind them that what they are doing is necessary. As simple and paternal as this may sound, it is a remarkably effective tool for draining tension from a productive but difficult interchange, giving the participants the confidence to continue. And once the discussion or meeting has ended, it is helpful to remind participants that the conflict they just engaged in is good for the team and not something to avoid in the future.

Other Tools   As mentioned earlier in this section, there are a variety of personality style and behavioral preference tools that allow team members to better understand one another. Because most of these include descriptions of how different types deal with conflict, they can be useful for helping people anticipate their approach or resistance to it. Another tool that specifically relates to conflict is the Thomas-Kilmann Conflict Mode Instrument, commonly referred to as the TKI.

It allows team members to understand natural inclinations around conflict so they can make more strategic choices about which approaches are most appropriate in different situations.

The Role of the Leader

One of the most difficult challenges that a leader faces in promoting healthy conflict is the desire to protect members from harm. This leads to premature interruption of disagreements, and prevents team members from developing coping skills for dealing with conflict themselves. This is not unlike parents who overprotect their children from quarrels or altercations with siblings. In many cases, it serves only to strain the relationships by depriving the participants of an opportunity to develop conflict management skills. It also leaves them hungry for resolution that never occurs.

Therefore, it is key that leaders demonstrate restraint when their people engage in conflict, and allow resolution to occur naturally, as messy as it can sometimes be. This can be a challenge because many leaders feel that they are somehow failing in their jobs by losing control of their teams during conflict.

Finally, as trite as it may sound, a leader's ability to personally model appropriate conflict behavior is essential. By avoiding conflict when it is necessary and productive—something many executives do—a team leader will encourage this dysfunction to thrive.

Connection to Dysfunction 3

How does all of this relate to the next dysfunction, the lack of commitment? By engaging in productive conflict and tapping into team members' perspectives and opinions, a team can confidently commit and buy in to a decision knowing that they have benefited from everyone's ideas.

DYSFUNCTION 3: LACK OF COMMITMENT

In the context of a team, commitment is a function of two things: clarity and buy-in. Great teams make clear and timely decisions and move forward with complete buy-in from every member of the team, even those who voted against the decision. They leave meetings confident that no one on the team is quietly harboring doubts about whether to support the actions agreed on.

The two greatest causes of the lack of commitment are the desire for consensus and the need for certainty:

- *Consensus.* Great teams understand the danger of seeking consensus, and find ways to achieve buy-in even when complete agreement is impossible. They understand that reasonable human beings do not need to get their way in order to support a decision, but only need to know that their opinions have been heard and considered. Great teams ensure that everyone's ideas are genuinely considered, which then creates a willingness to rally around whatever decision is ultimately made by the group. And when that

207

is not possible due to an impasse, the leader of the team is allowed to make the call.

- *Certainty.* Great teams also pride themselves on being able to unite behind decisions and commit to clear courses of action even when there is little assurance about whether the decision is correct. That's because they understand the old military axiom that *a* decision is better than *no* decision. They also realize that it is better to make a decision boldly and be wrong—and then change direction with equal boldness—than it is to waffle.

Contrast this with the behavior of dysfunctional teams that try to hedge their bets and delay important decisions until they have enough data to feel certain that they are making the right decision. As prudent as this might seem, it is dangerous because of the paralysis and lack of confidence it breeds within a team.

It is important to remember that conflict underlies the willingness to commit without perfect information. In many cases, teams have all the information they need, but it resides within the hearts and minds of the team itself and must be extracted through unfiltered debate. Only when everyone has put their opinions and perspectives on the table can the team confidently commit to a decision knowing that it has tapped into the collective wisdom of the entire group.

Regardless of whether it is caused by the need for consensus or certainty, it is important to understand that one of the greatest consequences for an *executive* team that does not commit to clear decisions is unresolvable discord deeper in the organization. More than any of the dysfunctions, this one creates dangerous ripple effects for subordinates. When an executive team fails to achieve buy-in from all team members, even if the disparities that exist seem relatively small, employees who report to those executives will inevitably clash when they try to interpret marching orders that are not clearly aligned with those of colleagues in other departments. Like a vortex, small gaps between executives high up in an organization become major discrepancies by the time they reach employees below.

A team that fails to commit ...
- Creates ambiguity among the team about direction and priorities
- Watches windows of opportunity close due to excessive analysis and unnecessary delay
- Breeds lack of confidence and fear of failure
- Revisits discussions and decisions again and again
- Encourages second-guessing among team members

A team that commits ...
- Creates clarity around direction and priorities
- Aligns the entire team around common objectives
- Develops an ability to learn from mistakes
- Takes advantage of opportunities before competitors do
- Moves forward without hesitation
- Changes direction without hesitation or guilt

Suggestions for Overcoming Dysfunction 3

How does a team go about ensuring commitment? By taking specific steps to maximize clarity and achieve buy-in, and resisting the lure of consensus or certainty. Here are a few simple but effective tools and principles.

Cascading Messaging   One of the most valuable disciplines that any team can adopt takes just a few minutes and is absolutely free. At the end of a staff meeting or off-site, a team should explicitly review the key decisions made during the meeting, and agree on what needs to be communicated to employees or other constituencies about those decisions. What often happens during this exercise is that members of the team learn that they are not all on the same page about what has been agreed upon and that they need to clarify specific outcomes before putting them into action. Moreover, they become clear on which of the decisions should remain confidential, and which must be communicated quickly and comprehensively. Finally, by leaving meetings clearly aligned with one another, leaders send a powerful and welcomed message to employees who have grown accustomed to receiving inconsistent and even contradictory statements from managers who attended the same meeting. (Minimum time required: 10 minutes.)

Deadlines   As simple as it seems, one of the best tools for ensuring commitment is the use of clear deadlines for when decisions will be made, and honoring those dates with discipline and rigidity. The worst enemy of a team that is susceptible to this dysfunction is ambiguity, and timing is one of the most critical factors that must be made clear. What is more, committing to deadlines for intermediate decisions and milestones is just as important as final deadlines, because it ensures that misalignment among team members is identified and addressed before the costs are too great.

Contingency and Worst-Case Scenario Analysis　A team that struggles with commitment can begin overcoming this tendency by briefly discussing contingency plans up front or, better yet, clarifying the worst-case scenario for a decision they are struggling to make. This usually allows them to reduce their fears by helping them realize that the costs of an incorrect decision are survivable, and far less damaging than they had imagined.

Low-Risk Exposure Therapy　Another relevant exercise for a commitment-phobic team is the demonstration of decisiveness in relatively low-risk situations. When teams force themselves to make decisions after substantial discussion but little analysis or research, they usually come to realize that the quality of the decision they made was better than they had expected. What is more, they learn that the decision would not have been much different had the team engaged in lengthy, time-consuming study. This is not to say that research and analysis are not necessary or important, but rather that teams with this dysfunction tend to overvalue them.

The Role of the Leader

More than any other member of the team, the leader must be comfortable with the prospect of making a decision that ultimately turns out to be wrong. And the leader must be constantly pushing the group for closure around issues, as well as adherence to schedules that the team has set. What the leader cannot do is place too high a premium on certainty or consensus.

Connection to Dysfunction 4

How does all of this relate to the next dysfunction, the avoidance of accountability? In order for teammates to call each other on their behaviors and actions, they must have a clear sense of what is expected. Even the most ardent believers in accountability usually balk at having to hold someone accountable for something that was never bought in to or made clear in the first place.

DYSFUNCTION 4: AVOIDANCE OF ACCOUNTABILITY

Accountability is a buzzword that has lost much of its meaning as it has become as overused as terms like *empowerment* and *quality*. In the context of teamwork, however, it refers specifically to the willingness of team members to call their peers on performance or behaviors that might hurt the team.

The essence of this dysfunction is the unwillingness of team members to tolerate the interpersonal discomfort that accompanies calling a peer on his or her behavior and the more general tendency to avoid difficult conversations. Members of great teams overcome these natural inclinations, opting instead to "enter the danger" with one another.

Of course, this is easier said than done, even among cohesive teams with strong personal relationships. In fact, team members who are particularly close to one another sometimes hesitate to hold one another accountable precisely because they fear jeopardizing a valuable personal relationship. Ironically, this only causes the relationship to deteriorate as team members begin to resent one another for not living up to expectations and for allowing the standards of the group to erode. Members of great teams improve their relationships by holding one another accountable, thus demonstrating that they respect each other and have high expectations for one another's performance.

As politically incorrect as it sounds, the most effective and efficient means of maintaining high standards of performance on a team is peer pressure. One of the benefits is the reduction of the need for excessive bureaucracy around performance management and corrective action. More than any policy or system, there is nothing like the fear of letting down respected teammates that motivates people to improve their performance.

Suggestions for Overcoming Dysfunction 4

How does a team go about ensuring accountability? The key to overcoming this dysfunction is adhering to a few classic management tools that are as effective as they are simple.

A team that avoids accountability ...
- Creates resentment among team members who have different standards of performance
- Encourages mediocrity
- Misses deadlines and key deliverables
- Places an undue burden on the team leader as the sole source of discipline

A team that holds one another accountable ...
- Ensures that poor performers feel pressure to improve
- Identifies potential problems quickly by questioning one another's approaches without hesitation
- Establishes respect among team members who are held to the same high standards
- Avoids excessive bureaucracy around performance management and corrective action

Publication of Goals and Standards A good way to make it easier for team members to hold one another accountable is to clarify publicly exactly what the team needs to achieve, who needs to deliver what, and how everyone must behave in order to succeed. The enemy of accountability is ambiguity, and even when a team has initially committed to a plan or a set of behavioral standards, it is important to keep those agreements in the open so that no one can easily ignore them.

Simple and Regular Progress Reviews A little structure goes a long way toward helping people take action that they might not otherwise be inclined to do. This is especially true when it comes to giving people feedback on their behavior or performance. Team members should regularly communicate with one another, either verbally or in written form, about how they feel their teammates are doing against stated objectives and standards. Relying on them to do so on their own, with no clear expectations or structure, is inviting the potential for the avoidance of accountability.

Team Rewards   By shifting rewards away from individual performance to team achievement, the team can create a culture of accountability. This occurs because a team is unlikely to stand by quietly and fail because a peer is not pulling his or her weight.

The Role of the Leader

One of the most difficult challenges for a leader who wants to instill accountability on a team is to encourage and allow the team to serve as the first and primary accountability mechanism. Sometimes strong leaders naturally create an accountability vacuum within the team, leaving themselves as the only source of discipline. This creates an environment where team members assume that the leader is holding others accountable, and so they hold back even when they see something that isn't right.

Once a leader has created a culture of accountability on a team, however, he or she must be willing to serve as the ultimate arbiter of discipline when the team itself fails. This should be a rare occurrence. Nevertheless, it must be clear to all team members that accountability has not been relegated to a consensus approach, but merely to a shared team responsibility, and that the leader of the team will not hesitate to step in when it is necessary.

Connection to Dysfunction 5

How does all of this relate to the next dysfunction, the inattention to results? If teammates are not being held accountable for their contributions, they will be more likely to turn their attention to their own needs, and to the advancement of themselves or their departments. An absence of accountability is an invitation to team members to shift their attention to areas other than collective results.

DYSFUNCTION 5: INATTENTION TO RESULTS

The ultimate dysfunction of a team is the tendency of members to care about something other than the collective goals of the group. An unrelenting focus on specific objectives and clearly defined outcomes is a requirement for any team that judges itself on performance.

It should be noted here that results are not limited to financial measures like profit, revenue, or shareholder returns. Though it is true that many organizations in a capitalist economic environment ultimately measure their success in these terms, this dysfunction refers to a far broader definition of results, one that is related to outcome-based performance.

Every good organization specifies what it plans to

achieve in a given period, and these goals, more than the financial metrics that they drive, make up the majority of near-term, controllable results. So, while profit may be the ultimate measure of results for a corporation, the goals and objectives that executives set for themselves along the way constitute a more representative example of the results it strives for as a team. Ultimately, these goals drive profit.

But what would a team be focused on other than results? Team status and individual status are the prime candidates:

- *Team status.* For members of some teams, merely being part of the group is enough to keep them satisfied. For them, the achievement of specific results might be desirable, but not necessarily worthy of great sacrifice or inconvenience. As ridiculous and dangerous as this might seem, plenty of teams fall prey to the lure of status. These often include altruistic nonprofit organizations that come to believe that the nobility of their mission is enough to justify their satisfaction. Political groups, academic departments, and prestigious companies are also susceptible to this dysfunction, as they often see success in merely being associated with their *special* organizations.

- *Individual status.* This refers to the familiar tendency of people to focus on enhancing their own positions or career prospects at the expense of their team. Though all human beings have an innate tendency toward self-preservation, a functional team must make the collective results of the group more important to each individual than individual members' goals.

As obvious as this dysfunction might seem at first glance, and as clear as it is that it must be avoided, it is important to note that many teams are simply not results focused. They do not live and breathe in order to achieve meaningful objectives, but rather merely to exist or survive. Unfortunately for these groups, no amount of trust, conflict, commitment, or accountability can compensate for a lack of desire to win.

Suggestions for Overcoming Dysfunction 5

How does a team go about ensuring that its attention is focused on results? By making results clear, and rewarding only those behaviors and actions that contribute to those results.

A team that is not focused on results ...
- Stagnates/fails to grow
- Rarely defeats competitors
- Loses achievement-oriented employees
- Encourages team members to focus on their own careers and individual goals
- Is easily distracted

A team that focuses on collective results ...
- Retains achievement-oriented employees
- Minimizes individualistic behavior
- Enjoys success and suffers failure acutely
- Benefits from individuals who subjugate their own goals/interests for the good of the team
- Avoids distractions

Public Declaration of Results   In the mind of a football or basketball coach, one of the worst things a team member can do is publicly guarantee that his or her team will win an upcoming game. In the case of an athletic team, this is a problem because it can unnecessarily provoke an opponent. For most teams, however, it can be helpful to make public proclamations about intended success.

Teams that are willing to commit publicly to specific results are more likely to work with a passionate, even desperate desire to achieve those results. Teams that say, "We'll do our best," are subtly, if not purposefully, preparing themselves for failure.

Results-Based Rewards   An effective way to ensure that team members focus their attention on results is to tie their rewards, especially compensation, to the achievement of specific outcomes. Relying on this alone can be problematic because it assumes that financial motivation is the sole driver of behavior. Still, letting someone take home a bonus merely for "trying hard," even in the absence of results, sends a message that achieving the outcome may not be terribly important after all.

The Role of the Leader

Perhaps more than with any of the other dysfunctions, the leader must set the tone for a focus on results. If team members sense that the leader values anything other than results, they will take that as permission to do the same for themselves. Team leaders must be selfless and objective, and reserve rewards and recognition for those who make real contributions to the achievement of group goals.

SUMMARY

As much information as is contained here, the reality remains that teamwork ultimately comes down to practicing a small set of principles over a long period of time. Success is not a matter of mastering subtle, sophisticated theory, but rather of embracing common sense with uncommon levels of discipline and persistence.

Ironically, teams succeed because they are exceedingly human. By acknowledging the imperfections of their humanity, members of functional teams overcome the natural tendencies that make trust, conflict, commitment, accountability, and a focus on results so elusive.

A NOTE
ABOUT TIME:
KATHRYN'S
METHODS

Kathryn understood that a strong team spends considerable time together, and that by doing so, they actually save time by eliminating confusion and minimizing redundant effort and communication. Added together, Kathryn and her team spent approximately eight days each quarter in regularly scheduled meetings, which amounts to fewer than three days per month. As little as this seems when considered as a whole, most management teams balk at spending this much time together, preferring to do "real work" instead.

Though there are actually many different ways to run a management team, Kathryn's methods are worth considering. Following is a description of how she ran her staff after her initial team-building off-sites and the significant investment in time that it required:

- Annual planning meeting and leadership development retreats (three days, off-site)

  Topics might include budget discussions, major strategic planning overview, leadership training, succession planning, and cascading messaging

- Quarterly staff meetings (two days, off-site)

  Topics might include major goal reviews, financial review, strategic discussions, employee performance discussions, key issue resolution, team development, and cascading messages

- Weekly staff meetings (two hours, on-site)

  Topics might include key activity review, goal progress review, sales review, customer review, tactical issue resolution, cascading messages

- Ad hoc topical meetings (two hours, on-site)

  Topics might include strategic issues that cannot be adequately discussed during weekly staff meetings

A SPECIAL TRIBUTE
TO TEAMWORK

As I was nearing the completion of this book, the horrible events of September 11, 2001, occurred. Amid the unfathomable tragedy of the situation and the amazing triumph of the country's response, a powerful and inspiring example of teamwork emerged—one that must be acknowledged here.

The men and women of the fire, rescue, and police departments in New York City, Washington, D.C., and Pennsylvania demonstrated that groups of people working together can accomplish what no assembly of mere individuals could ever dream of doing.

In emergency services professions like these, team members live and work together, developing bonds of trust that only families can rival. That allows them to engage in focused, unfiltered debate over the right course of action to take when every second is precious. As a result, they are able to commit quickly to unambiguous decisions under the most dangerous of circumstances, when most other human beings would demand more information before taking action. And with so much on the line, they don't hesitate to push their colleagues and hold them accountable for carrying their loads, knowing that even one team member slacking could cost lives. And finally, they have only one end in mind: protecting the lives and liberties of others.

The ultimate test of a great team is results. And considering that tens of thousands of people escaped from the World Trade Center towers in New York City and the Pentagon in Washington, D.C., there can be no doubt that the teams who risked, and lost, their lives to save them were extraordinary.

May God bless them all, as well as the victims and survivors they worked together to save.

ACKNOWLEDGMENTS

This book is the result of a team effort, not only during its writing but throughout my education and career. I would like to acknowledge those people who have been instrumental in my life.

First, I thank the head of my own first team, my wife, Laura. For your unconditional love, and your unwavering commitment to me and our boys, I cannot adequately describe my appreciation. And I thank Matthew and Connor, who will soon be able to read one of my books, though they'll certainly prefer Dr. Seuss. You give me so much joy.

Next, I offer sincere gratitude to my team at The Table Group, without whose ideas, editing, and passion this book would not have come to be. For Amy's graceful judgment and intuition, Tracy's extraordinary and unending diligence, Karen's kind support, John's stylish wisdom, Jeff's optimistic intelligence, Michele's insightfulness and humor, and Erin's youthful authenticity. I am constantly amazed and touched by the depth and quality of your commitment. You have helped me learn more about real teamwork than any group I have ever known, and I thank you for that.

I want to acknowledge the support and love of my parents. You have always given me the emotional safety net I needed to take risks and chase dreams. And you have given me so many things that you never had yourselves.

Thanks to my brother, Vince, for your passion, intensity, and concern.

And to my sister, Ritamarie, for your wisdom, love, and patience that mean more to me with every passing year.

And to the hundreds of cousins, aunts, uncles, and in-laws of mine—the Lencionis, the Shanleys, the Fanucchis, and the Gilmores. Thank you for your interest and kindness, which mean a lot to me even though I am far away from many of you.

Thanks to Barry Belli, Will Garner, Jamie and Kim Carlson, the Beans, the Elys, and the Patchs for your interest and friendship over the years.

I thank the many managers and mentors I've had during my career. Sally DeStefano for your confidence and graciousness. Mark Hoffman and Bob Epstein for your trust. Nusheen Hashemi for your enthusiasm. Meg Whitman and Ann Colister for your advice and counsel. And Gary Bolles for your encouragement and friendship.

I thank Joel Mena for your passion and love. Rick Robles for your coaching and teaching. And so many of the other teachers and coaches I had at Our Lady of Perpetual Help School, Garces High School, and Claremont McKenna College.

I thank the many clients whom I've worked with over the years for your trust and commitment to building a healthier organization.

I want to give special thanks to my agent, Jim Levine, for your humility and insistence on excellence, or as my wife says, for being "a humble butt-kicker." And to my editor, Susan Williams, for your enthusiasm and flexibility. Thanks to everyone at Jossey-Bass and Wiley for your persistence, support, and commitment.

Finally, and certainly most important of all, I give all thanks to God the Father, the Son, and the Holy Spirit for all that I am.

ABOUT THE AUTHOR

Patrick Lencioni is founder and president of The Table Group, a management consulting firm specializing in executive team development and organizational health. As a consultant and keynote speaker, he has worked with thousands of senior executives in organizations ranging from Fortune 500s and high-tech start-ups to universities and non-profits. Clients who have engaged his services include New York Life, Southwest Airlines, Sam's Club, Microsoft, Allstate, Visa, FedEx, and the U.S. Military Academy, West Point, to name a few. He is the author of five nationally recognized books, including the *New York Times* best-seller *The Five Dysfunctions of a Team* (Jossey-Bass, 2002).

Patrick lives in the San Francisco Bay Area with his wife, Laura, and their three sons, Matthew, Connor, and Casey.

To learn more about Patrick and The Table Group, please visit www.tablegroup.com.

Introducing the *Five Dysfunctions of a Team Workshop*
Based on the *New York Times* best-selling book
The Five Dysfunctions of a Team
by Patrick Lencioni

The Five Dysfunctions of a Team Workshop is a unique learning experience designed to help teams take their first steps toward greater cohesiveness and productivity. Using powerful exercises, teams will make significant progress in each of the five fundamentals introduced in this book: trust, conflict, commitment, accountability, and results. This innovative workshop, developed and field-tested by Patrick Lencioni and his firm, The Table Group, prompts teams to take their first steps toward real, lasting change.

Program materials include a comprehensive Facilitator's Guide, Participant Workbook, Team Assessment, poster, and video. The Facilitator's Guide contains everything you need to plan, conduct, and follow up a workshop. It is designed to be used by anyone who wants to help a team improve its performance, including internal and external consultants, team leaders, and managers and executives.

For more information please contact leadership@wiley.com or specialsales@wiley.com. If you are part of a government organization, please contact jskinner@wiley.com. If you would prefer to speak to one of our team consultants by phone, please call toll-free 1-866-888-5159.

Applying the Dysfunctions Model

Patrick Lencioni's company, The Table Group, offers teams additional products and services designed to improve team performance.

Dysfunctions Products

The Table Group has developed a flexible suite of tools around *The Five Dysfunctions of a Team*. The products are designed for rapid application and to bring about meaningful, relevant change.

Dysfunctions Consulting

The Table Group provides fast-paced, practical, and compelling consulting sessions to leaders and their teams. Consultants work with teams across a range of company sizes and industries, providing concrete tools and concepts that are immediately applicable within organizations.

For more information please visit
www.tablegroup.com